Theatre Administration

Francis Reid

Adam & Charles Black · London

First published 1983 by A & C Black (Publishers) Ltd
35 Bedford Row, London WC1R 4JH

© 1983 Francis Reid

Reid, Francis
    Theatre administration.
    1.   Theater management
    I.   Title
    792'.068   PN2053

    ISBN 0-7136-2368-3

Printed by BAS Printers Limited,
Over Wallop, Hampshire

Contents

Prologue

In 1979 I was offered the job of Administrator of a mixed programme theatre. It was in East Anglia and it was Georgian. It was desperately underfunded and a victim of a loss of self-confidence that had spread, inevitably, to audience, press, local authorities and the arts establishment. I hesitated. Not because there were problems or because I had never managed a theatre, but because it was too far from the sea. But I overcame my hang-up about tidal waters and took the job. Careers in theatre are rarely structured. Sometimes one has to choose between interesting work and simple survival. I have been hyper-lucky in that for over a quarter of a century I have survived by following the options that promised interest.

When trying to acquire any new skill I have always relied on reading books plus observation of cause and effect. From observation of the processes of administration in theatres great and grotty I had formed opinions and picked up a lot of the sort of useful background that is perhaps best described as 'street knowledge'. But my search of the bookshops and libraries was less rewarding. Certain areas like marketing and copyright had specialist manuals and there was a lot of writing on what might be called the ethics of arts administration: topics like the role of the arts in society and the role of the state in arts funding. I wanted a beginner's book on the basics of how the theatre world administers itself in terms of funding a show, manufacturing it and retailing to an audience many of whom probably would not realise that it might be an enjoyable experience if only they would give it a try. The only such book was out of print and, being restricted to the type of theatre that blossomed in the 1960s regional rep explosion, was really rather out of date.

So I had to fly my theatre by the seat of my pants. And as it was a Dakota rather than a Jumbo, we did not crash. My survival criteria were simple: buy cheap, sell dear and bang the drum. I have never understood the difference between arts and entertainment: I only know that between good and bad. I cannot bear the sound of country and western music but it had its place with Mozart, Melly, Pinter and Punk.

After a couple of invigorating years I was ready to return to the backstage where I belong, but before doing so I agreed to a suggestion that I ought to write the sort of book that I could not find on the bookshelves on the day that I became a theatre administrator. If some of the content seems like a statement of the obvious, it is because, in my experience both as a theatre worker and as audience, it is the obvious that is often the missing ingredient in so much arts administration.

What I cannot offer my readers is a structured plan for managing a theatre: there is no neat exercise which suggests that by performing tasks in a logical sequence a clear target can be achieved. The job of a theatre manager is akin to that of a juggler endeavouring to maintain some equilibrium between audiences, performers and funding bodies. Decisions have to be taken simultaneously, often in a spirit of faith mingled with hope, since much theatre business is undertaken in a climate bordering on technical insolvency. My aim therefore has been to indicate the basic administrative procedures required to ensure that an intended performance actually takes place, and to discuss the areas where decisions and actions are required to ensure the continuing existence of a theatre building or performing company.

For the words, I am indebted to all my friends in the theatre industry who supported my efforts at learning theatre administration by doing it, particularly the Chairman and dedicated staff of the Theatre Royal in Bury St Edmunds who supported me totally, even if some of my methods occasionally seemed a little unorthodox for an elegant Georgian playhouse in the care of the National Trust.

For help with the illustrations, I am particularly indebted to:
Arts Council of Great Britain, Barbican Arts Centre, BOCS, Bury St Edmunds Theatre Royal, Donmar, Eastern Arts Association, Equity, Greenwich Theatre, Malcolm Knight Productions, Norwich Theatre Royal, Performing Right Society, Pitlochry Festival Theatre, Royal Shakespeare Company, Scottish Arts Council, Scottish Opera, Theatrical Management Association, Ticketmaster.

Throughout this book, the word *actor* has been used to include all performers whether male or female; and in references to all personnel, the words *he* and *she* should be regarded as freely interchangeable. The world of theatre rejected discrimination of all kinds, including sex, long before such equality became either fashionable or a matter for legislation.

1   Theatres

The word *theatre* is used to describe both a performance and the place where that performance is given. The type of performance can generate various labels such as drama, opera, theatre of the absurd, theatre of cruelty, etc. The type of housing produces labels like opera house, street theatre, theatre-in-the-round, etc. And there is a further series of organisational labelling as mainstream theatre, alternative theatre, commercial theatre, subsidised theatre and so on.

But for administration purposes, the basic division into theatre *buildings* and theatre *companies* is convenient, with three possible permutations giving three reasonably distinct management situations:

*   Theatre buildings without companies
*   Theatre companies without buildings
*   Theatre buildings with companies.

Indeed one of the main concerns of theatre administration is the means by which buildings and companies are married together through the rental and touring systems which provide much of the theatre experience in the English-speaking world.

Theatres without companies

This category can include virtually every type of performance space, formal or informal. At one time, perhaps until about the mid 1960s, a division could be made fairly easily into theatres with open-ended runs as in London's West End or New York's Broadway, and the touring theatres with a predetermined length of run, usually a single week. However this simplicity has been changed by shifts in the performance pattern brought about partly by economics, partly by audience response, and partly by the emergence of companies playing a much wider range of types of performance. Today if a space has the basic requirements of assembly — chairs, electricity and a licence — then it is liable to host a performance. (Street theatre, of course, has neither chairs nor electricity and its relationships with the law are usually based on mutual tolerance. So, in administration terms, street theatre is a company rather than a building.)

To some extent the management structure of a theatre without a company is related to the type of production that the building houses, but it is mainly dependent on frequency of use.

Companies without theatres

Again the possible width is considerable. Traditionally such companies were assemblages of actors and staff brought together on an 'ad hoc' basis to mount a production either for London/Broadway or for tour. Many such tours were productions being 'run-in' on the way to the capital, or taking advantage of the publicity already generated by scoring a hit there. In England such tours have normally been after a West End run, but the geographical size of America has encouraged the touring of several companies concurrent with the Broadway run.

But in the last decade or so the pattern has changed. The preview system has largely ended 'trying out on the road' and any post-London productions are cast from a pool of touring stars generated not just by television but by television series. Similar casting is used for touring revivals of the mainstream theatre's successes of yesteryear — particularly thrillers and comedies, although there are occasional tours of classical plays nearly always chosen with an eye to the exam syllabus. Some regional companies, including several for opera and dance, are based in rehearsal rooms rather than theatres, but tour a circuit of theatres with whom they have developed a regular relationship with the support of the Arts Council Touring Department.

The most positive feature of the 1970s and 80s, however, is the explosive growth of what started as 'fringe' theatre and has become known as 'alternative' theatre. This was made possible by the ending of the Lord Chamberlain's censorship of plays: not because they would have necessarily been refused licences, but because the creative process of so much alternative theatre would not have fitted in with the formal script submission process of the old censorship's administration.

With emphasis shifting from text towards music and movement, a broadening of acting style, and an approach to scenography that combines flexibility with economy, alternative theatre has grown closer to, and combined with, concert packages to widen the range of available touring productions. A range which not only adapts to all sorts of theatre buildings, conventional and unconventional, formal and informal, but also attracts new audiences.

The management structure of theatreless companies depends on a number of factors: size is perhaps the most obvious one, but the degree of formality of the operation is also a strong influence.

Theatres with companies

Germany is the country with the most highly developed network of building-based theatre companies. Each town with a population of around 100,000 upwards has a theatre organisation comprising theatre buildings, actors, singers, dancers, orchestra and production staff. Each civic theatre is a complete unit capable of building, rehearsing, and performing operas, musicals, concerts, ballets and drama within its own premises. The size of this organisation naturally varies with the size of the city and consequently with the amount of finance that can be provided from the city and other local authorities. This type of performance provision exists throughout Eastern Europe and there is a similar if not quite so comprehensive situation in other countries of Europe — adapted to local conditions, particularly in Scandinavian countries where there are population concentrations with this type of theatre, plus areas of scattered population that can only be reached by touring.

In Britain, throughout the 1920s and 30s, there was a growing repertory movement with building-based companies being set up in a number of towns. But it was not until the establishment of the Arts Council of Great Britain during the 1939-45 war, and the consequent general acceptance of the idea of public subsidy, that these repertory theatres could be developed into a regional network. The decision to have a civic playhouse was not imposed by central government or its agencies: the initial impetus had to come from the community, whereupon funds were provided by the Arts Council to assist with building a theatre and maintaining a production company. In most cases that impetus was provided by an informal group of concerned enthusiastic activists rather than by a formal initiative by their local authority. And, particularly in the earlier years of regional theatre, it was central Arts Council rather than local government that set the pace in providing funding.

Whereas the Central European civic theatres are primarily lyric theatres performing a great deal of opera and other musical theatre, the British civic theatres are almost entirely drama houses, producing only the occasional small-scale musical.

Theatres with their own resident production companies almost require two separate administrative staffs to handle the management of the building and the management of the acting company. However, particularly in the smaller organisations, there is a degree of overlap with the result that some sharing of responsibilities, and therefore some small economy in staffing numbers, is possible.

Types of theatre

Theatre, whether building or company, falls into a number of possible categories based on type of ownership, funding and programme.

Commercial theatre

There is no longer such a thing as a completely commercial theatre building operating in a free market to produce a return on investment comparable

with other types of property rental. The London West End theatres operated by private or public companies come closest to commercial viability
but, in virtually every case, their asset potential for redevelopment exceeds
the return from operating a successful theatre on the site. That theatres
remain on these sites is mainly a result of planning restrictions, although
happily there is also quite a considerable degree of theatre loving philan-
thropy among certain leaseholders. This extends to the occasional free-
holder but there is a tendency, inevitable and understandable, for the
freeholds to be acquired by property development companies. In both London and New York, redevelopment permission has usually been given only
if the new building incorporates a theatre. In London particularly, this has
tended to result in theatres with technical shortcomings and lacking in
audience appeal: consequently they are rarely viable.

The Theatres Trust was set up in 1976 to safeguard theatre buildings
threatened by development, but so far it has had to remain a watchdog body
without financial teeth.

Outside London, the once-powerful commercial touring theatre circuits
have vanished. Of the two big chains, Howard & Wyndham have disappeared completely, while Moss Empires retain only the Bristol Hippod-
rome and that is run with support from the local authority and arts funding
bodies. In many cases the old touring theatres have been acquired by local
authorities and are now run either directly or through trusts as part of the
new middle-scale and large-scale touring circuits.

Commercial theatre companies on the other hand still play quite a force-
ful role in the theatre economy. In the West End and on Broadway, each
production is financed as a separate entity by investors who put up high risk
capital. The risk of them losing most or all of this capital is very high . . .
never mind showing a profitable return on that capital. So why do these
'backers' or 'angels' invest? Well, if a show is a hit, the profits can be very
high indeed — perhaps enough to average out some of the big losses for a
regular investor. And there is a certain amount of glamour attached to being
an angel.

Many plays, particularly single set comedies and thrillers, are still toured
on a commercial basis. Investors are not normally required because the
touring management company endeavours to cover the basic risk by seeking
a financial guarantee from each touring theatre, amounting to the weekly
running costs plus a proportion of production costs. However, as the touring
theatres are normally risking their own subsidised finances in providing
these guarantees, it is perhaps a rather fine shading of language to describe
such tours as completely commercial.

Trust theatres

Outside the commercial sector, most theatre companies and many buildings operate as non-profit distributing companies, frequently as trusts with charitable status. The directors are unpaid respectable citizens with an interest in theatre, plus nominees of the various bodies providing finance for the operation. These nominees may attend the meetings as directors, assesors, or observers according to the constitution of a particular trust and the standard practice of the body that they represent.

Local authority theatres

Some theatre buildings and a few building-based companies are directly managed by the local authority. However such authorities are virtually never in the business of managing companies other than those resident in their own theatres. Local authority ownership of theatres began mainly in seaside resorts where entertainment is a necessary amenity to attract the tourists who form an essential part of the resort's economy. As traditional forms of commercial theatre financing collapsed, some other authorities took over the direct management of theatres, regarding them as necessary social amenities on a par with public libraries, galleries, museums, swimming baths and sports facilities of all kinds.

An appropriate council committee oversees the operation. This is often Recreation and Amenities or may be others such as Libraries and Arts according to the committee structure of a particular authority. Day to day management is in the hands of the officers of the appropriate council department for which there is no standard title: Leisure Services, Leisure and Recreation, Leisure and Amenities, Recreation and Amenities, Tourism and Entertainment, Publicity and Entertainment are just some of the permutations in use.

Arts centre theatres

The term 'arts centre' is frequently used to cover large comprehensive arts operations like London's Barbican or New York's Lincoln Centre which include major conventional theatres. However the term is used here for the smaller centres which have usually been adapted from warehouses, chapels, fire stations, post offices and the like, and which include some sort of performance area with basic staging facilities. The performances of theatre type productions are likely to be occasional and to include a goodly proportion of amateur work. The professional drama input is likely to be mainly single nights or part weeks by alternative theatre companies. Arts centres normally operate as registered educational charities, usually run by a non-profit distributing company with a voluntary board including assessors appointed by bodies contributing to the funding. In this respect they are rather like the trust theatre category but, in the case of arts centres, theatre usually constitutes a contributing rather than a major role in the operation.

University theatres

Some university theatres exist, at least partly, as a teaching facility for their drama departments. Others are there purely as a cultural amenity to enhance the quality of life for students and faculty. All are open to the public and indeed intended to have a positive effect on relationships between town and gown. Most have their maintenance and basic overheads covered by university funds while receiving subsidy towards their production costs from the Arts Council and/or Regional Arts Associations.

Festival theatres

Some theatre organisations exist to give a limited number of performances of very high quality, often in a location selected for its association with the works to be staged or the personalities involved. The company is usually recruited for the festival season although a skeleton administration is required on a permanent basis for forward planning.

Amateur theatres

Most amateur societies play in rented theatres and halls. Others however have their own premises where they can rehearse and stage their productions. Administration usually falls upon a small dedicated committee or even just upon one noble Hon. Sec. A few societies, such as the Maddermarket in Norwich, maintain a programme nearly as full as a regional professional repertory company. To do this they may employ a professional director/administrator, and often a designer and/or technician as well.

Occasional theatres

At one time any hall with a stage could be pressed into service as a theatre. With the growth of experimental drama, a stage is no longer essential. There are therefore a large number of halls which become theatres on an occasional basis, despite problems with licensing. Companies visiting such spaces assume nothing — no personnel (management or technical) and no equipment.

Controlling bodies

A theatre building or company may operate under the personal direction of its owners, whether a sole proprietor or a partnership. However this is rarely done because of the financial risk to the owner's or partners' other financial assets in the event of theatrical failure. Liability is therefore normally limited in one of the following ways.

Board of shareholders

A public or, more commonly, private limited liability company whose directors represent shareholders and are elected by them. There is normally a mixture of executive and non-executive directors. It is quite common for these directors to be the only shareholders — the main purpose in operating in this way being to create a separate entity which can go bust while leaving the owners personally solvent. Operation as a limited company is controlled by complex law and there is an obligation to make statutory returns under the Companies Acts.

Boards of trustees

A non-profit distributing theatre operation is normally constituted as a company limited by guarantee, with the liability of members in the event of bankruptcy being limited to a nominal sum, usually one pound — although continuing to trade while knowingly insolvent could result in charges of criminal negligence against the directors. Additionally, the benefits to be derived from charitable status usually make registration with the charity commissioners desirable, the benefits including rating relief and tax recovery on covenanted donations. A company limited by guarantee has to fulfill the same obligations as any other company, including the submission of annual returns. An important feature of the board of such a company is its public accountability. Its financial integrity must not just be impeccable, it must be seen to be so. In addition to directors with theatrical interest and experience, there should be representatives of all bodies assisting with revenue funding. Ideally such representatives should see their function in the dual capacity of supporting their board's application for a grant, followed by overseeing the expenditure of the sum allocated. Their appointment should be seen as an interface.

Local authority committees

A local authority comprises elected members and the professional officers who carry out the minuted decisions of these members. When a theatre is directly managed by a local authority, its policy is laid down by the appropriate committee drawn from the elected members. The theatre's budget is incorporated within the estimates prepared by that committee and approved by the full council. The decisions are then implemented by the officers. The public accountability of a local authority is impeccable: however the degree

```
                    STATISTICS 1979/80

Total audience.......................................54,172
Overall 61% but growing throughout the year

      179 performances of 48 attractions (professional)
       76 performances of 18 attractions (amateur)
      ———                  ——
      255 performances of 66 attractions (TOTAL)


      Professional Drama...........................73 perfs
      Pantomime....................................45
      Amateur Plays................................26
      Amateur Musicals.............................24
      Country & West...............................13
      Young Childrens Shows........................14
      Amateur Dance................................12
      Professional Dance........................... 1
      Jazz......................................... 4
      Folk......................................... 3
      Opera........................................ 2
      Classical Concerts........................... 5
      Rock......................................... 1
      Miscellaneous................................32

─────────────────────────────────────────────────────────

COSTS
      Overheads                    £49,000
      Productions                   72,000
                                   ————————
                                  £121,000
                                                SURPLUS
INCOME
      Local Authorities             31,750       £9,000
      Eastern Arts Association       8,250
      Friends                        2,500
      Catering & Programmes          2,500
      Box-Office & Rentals          85,000
                                   ————————
                                  £130,000

ALLOCATION OF SURPLUS

      Elimination of Brought Forward Deficit............ £6,000
      Transfer to Renewals Fund.........................  2,000
      Carry Forward.....................................  1,000
                                                        ————————
                                                         £9,000
```

Public accountability is a major responsibility of the Board of Management of a theatre organisation receiving income from public funds. This public accountability includes making financial information available in an easily digested form. This sheet of statistics was made available to the press, to enquirers and to the annual open meeting of the Friends organisation in an effort to explain the position of the Theatre Royal, Bury St Edmunds.

of theatre expertise, interest or even concern among committee members is a matter of some chance.

Operation of a management company

Constitution

The backbone of a company is its 'Memorandum and Articles of Association'. This is drawn up by a solicitor at the time of the company's formation and takes account of the nature of the company's operation, with the nature of business stated as flexibly as possible to allow for future variations. By far the largest number of theatrical companies are limited by guarantee and do not have a share capital. Indeed operation in this mode is virtually a pre-requisite for receiving subsidy.

Statutory returns

Under company law, every limited company is required to submit an annual return to the Registrar of Companies, using a prescribed form. This return must be accompanied by a simple annual report and a set of certified accounts.

Minutes

The decisions of the company as taken by directors at meetings are recorded in the minutes. There are three basic categories of minutes:

* Mandatory minutes such as resolutions to adopt annual accounts or authorise bank account signatories etc.

* Authorising minutes which record the directors' approval of action to be taken by the company's employees. (Such authorisation may also take the form of retrospective approval.)

* Recording minutes which precis the discussion. These are partly just for the record, but principally for the information of directors who were absent from the meeting.

For ease of reference, the minutes should be set out in a standard format corresponding to the agenda. It is common practice to number each minute and there is a strong case for numbering them consecutively from the beginning of each financial year rather than from the beginning of each meeting. Whether or not this is done, it is certainly essential to assign a consecutive number to each meeting to simplify reference.

Agenda

The last item on any set of minutes is the date of the next meeting. Monthly boards usually meet on a fixed date such as the fourth Wednesday, but boards who meet less frequently are likely to vary the date. Because of this it is essential, apart from general efficiency, that minutes are circulated as soon as possible after a meeting. One of the most common of director's moans is that they receive minutes together with the agenda for the next meeting, at a time so close to that meeting that they already have another engagement arranged. So missing one meeting has a knock-on effect resulting in missing several. And it must be remembered that most theatre board members are unpaid volunteers.

The memorandum and articles of association of the company specify the notice to be given in calling the annual general meeting, and this is normally three weeks. The agenda for such a meeting is restricted to such formalities as:

* Consideration of director's annual report and statement of accounts.

* Election of directors.

* Election and remuneration of auditors.

The agenda of normal meetings should be circulated at least a week before, accompanied whenever possible by supporting papers. Only simple papers such as up-to-date financial results should be tabled at meetings: it is difficult to absorb the contents of policy papers during the course of a discussion.

Conduct of meetings

A good board meeting needs just enough formality in its proceedings to ensure that:

* Anyone with something positive to say gets a chance to say it.

* People speak only one at a time.

* Decisions are minuted.

* Resolutions are formally proposed and seconded.

If the meeting is conducted in an over-formal manner with inflexible procedural rules, the contributions from members tend to take on an air of policy statements pronounced from entrenched positions. Success lies largely with the chair who, like all good leaders (including theatre administrators) should carry an air of ultimate authority without ever being seen to exert it. The best decisions are those reached by consensus without formal vote.

To assist the smooth running of a board meeting, the chairman should hold a preliminary briefing discussion with the theatre's artistic and administrative heads. It is likely that many, perhaps most, of the board members will be inexperienced in the complex ways of theatre and they will require some guidance from the chair, as well as from the policy papers submitted by the administration. However it is to be hoped that the theatre's top professionals will enjoy regular discussion with their chairman as well as support. The relationship is rather like that between the chairman and manager of a football club. When that is strong, the results usually improve!

Management and other sub-committees

If the board meets infrequently, say less than about eight times per year, it may be desirable to consider having a smaller management committee to take interim decisions. Sub-committees may be formed to deal with areas such as finance, sponsorship, buildings, programming, etc. But these are time consuming for the professional administration to service, and the main board have been known to assume, with some justification, that they are merely rubber stamping decisions made by an inner caucus. Moreover is detailed decision making really a function of a theatrical board of directors? Should they not perhaps just concentrate on:

* Appointing a professional management in whom they have faith, and terminating that contract if they lose faith.
* Setting broad policy outlines, artistically and financially.
* Monitoring performance.
* Overseeing public accountability.
* Fulfilling legal obligations.

2 Staffs

All members of the staff running a theatre company or building are cogs in a management structure. Decisions on cost-effectiveness are required from all workers in all departments 'backstage' and 'front-of-house' — to use the terminology of the theatre world's classic divide. The nature and number of the decisions just does not permit the 'management and workers' approach that is satisfactory for other industries.

The essence of a management structure is the breaking down of responsibilities into defined logical areas, operating within a framework of agreed (not imposed) budgets and schedules.

The key to successful management is communication. Communication upwards, downwards and sideways. There has to be a hierarchy but this hierarchy should be implicit rather than evident: it is only there for the occasions when things get out of hand and a conflict has to be resolved by instructions rather than consensus discussion. Theatre has always been rather good at this. Apart from the matter of actors' billing, theatre people, front and back, are not status conscious. While the best theatres tend to be run by dictators, their personalities are such that they are rarely seen to be wielding power.

Staffing structure naturally varies with the size and type of a theatre operation and various options will become more apparent in later chapters considering specialised departments.

The permanent staff of a smallish theatre without its own company but relying on touring companies to provide a mixed programme might be restricted to Administrator, House Manager, Secretary, Box Office Manager and Assistant in the 'front-of-house' with a Stage Manager and Electrician 'backstage'. (Usherettes, bar staff and stage crew being part-time.) The first addition for a slightly larger theatre is likely to be an executive for press and publicity. For a theatre company without its own theatre, the staff might well be as small as Artistic Director (Producer), Business Manager, Production Manager and Secretary. Unless the company has a high level of activity including several simultaneous productions, other functions — even press and publicity — might well be sub-contracted or freelances employed as required. A producing theatre having its own company naturally requires the largest staff: Artistic Director, Administrator, Theatre Manager, House Manager, Box Office Manager and staff, Accounting Officer and staff, Catering Manager, a marketing and press department involving several people, and a Production Manager heading up a considerable workshop operation. Plus the actors and stage management under the immediate care of a Company Manager.

Job titles

Theatre jobs tend to be given rather grand names in line with the general ballyhoo that is an integral part of theatre. Several titles, particularly manager and administrator, are often prefaced with 'general' for no really logical reason, although it is not unknown right through the theatre industry for an inflated job title to be offered in compensation for an inadequate salary.

(General) Intendant   This German title is included because it is the one and only designation that leaves no doubt as to where each and every buck stops. Intendants are responsible for all artistic and business aspects of their theatre's operation.

Director   Can be used for a person having total control, but this can be confusing because it is the standard (union approved) designation in theatre, film and television for the person who controls the creative work of the actor and production team in the interpretation of the script. Further confusion arises with members of the board of directors of the controlling company.

Managing Director   Is only useable in the case of a commercial company since the directors of non-profit-distributing companies are normally prevented from receiving any fees or salaries from the company.

Producer   Formerly the person who directed the actors. Now established, particularly in commercial theatre, as the packager of a show: the person who brings together script, theatre, director, possibly the star(s), but certainly the money.

Artistic Director   Responsible for programme structure and performance standards.

(General) Manager   Oversees all business aspects including the preparation and control of budgets, accountancy, staff, and the day to day running of the theatre. In theatres without companies, may be responsible for selecting and negotiating the programme from available production packages.

(General) Administrator   Might, rather cynically, be defined as the more fashionable word for management. But perhaps implies the degree of positive artistic involvement which was expressed rather well by the late Sir David Webster when he defined his duties as General Administrator of the Royal Opera House as 'creating the conditions in which the aims and capabilities of the artists could be more fully realised and the best possible performances presented'. The Arts Council's 1971 'Report on the Training of Administrators' develops this idea, suggesting that the administrator creates 'a framework in which the artistic product can flourish with a minimum of inconvenience to the artistic creator of the product' by one who 'can dream along with the artistic director, but who can also possess the ability to translate ideas into figures and back again into ideas'. The administrator is an *enabler*.

Artistic Administrator   Occasionally used for the person who controls the total operation of a theatre without its own acting company. However the word 'artistic' is generally implied rather than stated in the administration of such a theatre.

(Arts and) Entertainment Manager   This and similar designations are sometimes used for the general management of theatres directly controlled by local authorities.

Note: From this point onwards, I propose to adopt the term Administrator to include General Manager and all variations on the Entertainments Manager theme. Thus, unless noted otherwise, a company will be assumed to have an Artistic Director and an Administrator, while a building has an Administrator. The degree of artistic responsibility of the administrator will therefore vary, but a considerable degree of artistic concern can be assumed.

Theatre Manager   When the administrator has the width of policy making involvement implied in the above administrative definition, a deputy is required to relieve the chief of day to day executive responsibilities to allow concentration on wider issues. The logical words *deputy* or *assistant* make many people feel that their enquiries are being dealt with by a subordinate of insufficient importance. Therefore the title theatre manager is frequently used for this position.

(and) Licensee   Most licences to operate a theatre building, particularly the Magistrates Licence for music, singing and dancing, and the local authority's licence under the Theatres Act, can be issued only to an individual, not to a company. The nominated senior person, usually the administrator or theatre manager, then has the words *and licensee* appended to his title, particularly on letterheads, posters and programmes.

House Manager   Supervises the domestic arrangements of the audience areas, including staffing and cleaning. Supervises the front-of-house arrangements for each performance, paying particular attention to audience welfare.

Marketing Officer/Manager   An integrated approach to marketing is a relatively new concept in the theatre world. Where the term is used as a job title, it usually implies a coordinated publicity and selling effort of productions selected by the artistic direction. Arts marketing departments have a long way to go before they achieve the control over product decisions that is common in other industries.

Publicity Officer/Manager   Responsible for all advertising and print including posters, leaflets and programmes.

Press Officer/Manager   Responsible for all liaison with the media (press, television and radio) in an endeavour to secure editorial mention.

Press and Publicity Officer/Manager   Publicity and Press duties may be combined, but the functions are separate and it is essential to be meticulous in having separate dealings with the editorial and advertising departments of newspapers and magazines.

Public Relations/Public Affairs   These terms are occasionally used but PR has been so frequently satirised, particularly on television, that the term has lost much of its credibility in the eyes of the theatre world and has come to be regarded with some cynicism by the media.

Box Office Manager   Responsible for the sale of all tickets whether by mail, telephone, agents or over the counter in the theatre. Prepares daily returns of all tickets sold for current and advance performances. Balances these sales against all monies received whether in the form of cash, cheques or credit cards.

Catering/Bars Management   Whereas a small theatre can survive on a Head Barman supervised by the House Manager, the catering operation may become a separately managed department in a larger theatre with more sophisticated front of house facilities. On the other hand, the catering may be let out to a concessionaire rather than managed 'in-house'.

Finance/Accounting   Every theatre organisation requires internal daily book-keeping. If the system is properly set up, the administrator can interpret the trend of the figures and get a quick comparison between actual and budgeted income and expenditure. The formal accounts can then be prepared by an external firm of accountants. It is only the largest organisations that require an accounts department to carry out the whole process under a qualified manager who is a member of the management team advising the administrator.

Production Manager   From the administrative point of view, the key member of the technical operations team is the person responsible for the control of the production budget. The normal title in companies, whether or not they are resident in their own theatre, is Production Manager.

Technical Manager   This term is coming into general useage, particularly in theatres without companies, for the senior member of the stage operations staff. However the older term Resident Stage Manager is still in use and London's West End has many theatres still sticking to the traditional division into Master Carpenter responsible for stage, flys, props, etc., and Chief Electrician responsible for stage lighting and electrical engineering systems throughout the building. Both carpenter and electrician have equal status and report to the theatre manager. It is only the biggest theatres that have a separate maintenance department: normal practice is for the stage technicians to maintain the entire building, calling in outside contractors when necessary.

It must be emphasised that these are only some of the more common job titles. Indeed most theatre organisations are flexible enough to adapt their division of labour to fit the special talents of their personnel at any given time. Furthermore, the nature of any theatre operation, indeed the nature of 'theatre' itself, is constantly changing and this requires a fluid approach to both the nature and the name of each job.

Note: There are a number of backstage job titles and terms which an administrator needs to understand as part of 'theatre language': some of the more frequently used have been included in the glossary, on p. 144.

3 Capital funding

Funds for theatres may be classified under the standard financial headings of *capital* and *income*. Income is discussed in chapters 4 and 5.

With a few exceptions, theatres do not have capital reserves. Calculation of subsidy is based by most funding bodies on the principle of *deficit budgeting* whereby funds are made available to cover the projected annual shortfall between operating costs and income from all sources.

There are a few exceptions. Cambridge Arts Theatre, for example, has a sizeable endowment fund which generates investment income. This is not entirely to that theatre's advantage since it allows the local authority to restrict its assistance to a level below that which it might be expected to contribute. The existence of an endowment fund, however, does give a theatre some added flexibility in its operations, not to mention an attractive measure of independence.

Norwich Theatre Royal, through a combination of size, location and aggressive marketing, has been able to produce operating surpluses for several years. Since the local authority have not withdrawn support, the Theatre Royal Trust have been able to build up considerable capital reserves, allowing the income from this capital to accumulate as an insurance against any future reversals of fortune. They have been able to use some of these reserves to redecorate and re-equip the building. By the end of the 1981/82 season, despite spending some £197,000 on renovations and building extensions, there remained some £400,000 in the reserve which had accumulated over the previous ten years.

Theatre buildings and equipment suffer considerable wear and tear in both the audience and technical areas. Most of this is best dealt with on a rolling basis with provision in the budgets of both buildings and companies for annual expenditure on repairs and maintenance. Inevitably however there will be major items of re-equipping and development — computer lighting controls and box office systems for example — which are too expensive to deal with in one financial year. Since so many funding bodies discourage the accumulation of funds over several years to meet major contingencies, these frequently have to be dealt with by other means.

Appeals are an almost inevitable component of the capital funding exercise for a major project. Sponsorship is possible for something as tangible as a concrete building extension, although sponsors tend to favour theatrical productions rather than buildings. There is an 'Arts Council Housing the Arts Fund' which can provide a proportion of the required funds to prime the pump for contribution from other sources. Many capital improvements lead to the sort of savings in operational costs that can justify repayment from future revenue. Borrowing is generally too expensive to service, but if a theatre is otherwise succeeding in balancing its books, anticipated operational savings may justify a deficit in the short term. There is also the possibility of a local authority agreeing to an interest free loan — Bury St Edmunds District Council made available to their local theatre trust £10,000 for a new lighting control, interest free, repayable in five annual instalments of £2,000. The reasoning was that, at best, increased efficiency would reduce the rate of increase in the theatre's annual revenue requirements and, at worst, the council would have to increase their own annual subsidy to enable the theatre to maintain its repayments. Either way it was a neat political solution to the problem of keeping a civic amenity in business without having to make a supplementary grant of £10,000 available in a year when public sector finance was under pressure from central government.

West End

Each West End or Broadway show is financed as a separate entity. A producing management assembles a package of script, cast and production team to present the show in a rented theatre. Capital is subscribed by investors who are attracted by the apparent audience prospects of the package. In the case of an established producing management, their track record will play a large part in influencing investors to take the risk. The capital sum raised must be sufficient to cover all production costs: that is, all expenditure up to the first performance, including the 'physical production' of scenery, costumes, etc., plus rehearsal salaries, printing, publicity and the cost of getting in to the theatre and rehearsing there. There should also be sufficient money to nurse the play through the opening weeks while it (hopefully) builds an audience.

The producer takes a weekly management fee but his real return comes if and when the show recoups its production capital. Any initial operating surpluses are returned weekly to the investors until they have recouped their original investment. Thereafter the profits are split between producer and investors, normally with the producer taking 40% and the investors sharing 60%.

Many productions fail and close without recovering any of their production costs whatsoever. Some stagger on making a partial recoupment of their capital. The few that become hits can show substantial gains for their investors. Success breeds success: a hit play can generate valuable subsidiary

Weekly
account for a
small West
End play.

```
                     Michael Ramsbottom Productions

        "Turn to the Wind"  at the Royal Holborn Theatre

        RUNNING ACCOUNT for WEEK 12 (week ending September 19th, 1981)


        INCOME                        EXPENDITURE

        BOX OFFICE TAKINGS            SALARIES
                                      Artists.............. £1580
        Monday........ £1,232         Company & Stage Man..   392
        Tuesday........  1,482        Wardrobe.............    95
        Wednesday......  1,489        Holiday reserve......   120 ... 2187
        Thursday.......  1,153
        Friday.........  2,237        Theatre Staff
        Saturday..Mat..    543        Management & Box Off.   620
        Saturday..Eve..  2,932        Stage & Electrics....   742
                                      Other staff..........   874 ... 2236
                       £11,068
                                      National Insurance ...........   522

                                      THEATRE CONTRA
                                      Rental..............  1270
                                      Lighting & Heating..   227
                                      Miscellaneous.......   495 ... 1992

                                      PUBLICITY
                                      Bills & Signs.......   390
                                      Newspapers..........   325
                                      Press Agent.........    50 ...  775

                                      HIRES .........................  373

                                      MANAGEMENT FEE.................  400

                                      ACCOUNTANCY ...................   50

                                      INSURANCE .....................   20

                                      ROYALTIES
                                      Author..............   664
                                      Director............   221
                                      Designer............    50
                                      Lighting Designer...    25
                                      Eastshire Theatre...   166.... 1126

                                      STAGE,WARDROBE & SUNDRY EXPENSES 226

                                      RECASTING & REPLACEMENT RESERVE 200

                                      NET PROFIT FOR WEEK............  961


              £11,068                                         £11,068


        FINANCIAL POSITION TO DATE
        CAPITAL SUBSCRIBED.............. £30,000      Keppel, Wilson & Co,
                                                     Chartered Accountants,
        RUNNING PROFITS TO DATE.........  14,582     999 Trafalgar Mews,
        PRODUCTION COSTS ...............  25,327     London, WC.2.
        NET LOSS TO DATE ...............  10,745     24th September 1981.
```

rights. Even one which has struggled along and barely or even failed to
recoup generates for its producer a share in the royalties from future
regional and amateur rights. And there are always the film rights, even if
not much more than the title finally reaches the screen.

As production costs escalate with inflation, an investor's potential losses
have become much larger. In times of high interest rates, theatre investment

looks particularly unattractive. There is an inevitable tendency to play safe and the gap has widened between instant success and instant failure with less scope for nursing along the production which does not immediately 'take off' and play to substantial houses. Many West End productions now originate in the subsidised regional theatres where the bulk of the production costs are met from Arts Council and other funds. They are then only transferred to London if their success is established. This system is particularly appealing to authors and so puts plays with private investment at a further disadvantage.

Theatre Investment Fund

The Theatre Investment Fund (TIF) was set up in 1975 in an attempt to prime the investment pump. Its initial capital of £250,000 has been eroded by about half in seven years — by the standards of West End investment, this is success indeed! TIF will only advance 10 to 20% of a production and in 1982 could only invest in shows with a production cost ceiling of £110,000. Its aims are to have £5 million, with the government subscribing £2 million and private sources the remainder. It would then be prepared to invest up to a level of 49% in a project.

Working capital

Outside London, very few theatres have very much in the way of working capital in the traditional industrial sense. The buildings are probably rented and if they are owned have little asset value: a building whose use and site potential are severely restricted by planning law is poor security for a mortgage. Advance bookings generate a certain amount of cash flow and the banking system is frequently called upon to bridge the gap until the next instalment of an Arts Council or other subsidy is received.

Deficit financing does not exactly encourage thrift.

4   Earned income

The income to fund a theatre operation is of two distinct types: *earned* and *awarded*. The term 'unearned' is in regular use to describe the latter, but can confuse because it implies income from investments. 'Non-earned' is a better term but has the wrong kind of charitable overtones for a theatre operation which should be *awarded* public money because of the importance of its contribution to society. Moreover the administrative procedures to 'earn' the award of a subsidy are jolly hard work!

The primary function of a theatre is performance and therefore the primary source of earnings is box-office income from the sale of seats.

To help the audience enjoy an evening at the theatre and perhaps assist their appreciation of the performance, a theatre can undertake a number of auxiliary activities such as catering, publishing and sales of theatre related items. These activities may generate profits which can be classified as secondary income.

Another source of secondary income is commercial activities unrelated to the theatre activity but introduced purely with an eye to generating profits which can be applied to the primary theatre operation.

Box office

A theatre seat is rather like an aircraft seat: the value of the empties disappears as completely on curtain-up as on take-off. These seats are the ultimate in dated perishable goods: they just cannot be left in the fridge and sold tomorrow. Box office income can therefore be subject to wild fluctuations. There are, of course, attempts made to overcome these fluctuations by the use of specialised sales techniques to be discussed in a later chapter. But box office income is certainly the most variable figure in theatre finance and its prediction subject to procedures which must invariably take into account a considerable amount of intuition and luck.

A major problem arising from the fluctuation in seat prices is the knock-on effect on other income. A drop in audiences automatically results in a drop in sales of programmes, ice creams, drinks, etc. If that drop in secondary income fails to occur with a drop in box office, then the theatre must be running the sort of inefficient operation where the bars are unable to cope with a full house during the interval!

Low seat sales have various other knock-on effects. Image suffers. Audi-

The price of your ticket only <u>helps</u> pay for the performance you are seeing tonight.

YOU PAY FOR
50%

SCOTTISH ARTS COUNCIL
26%

LOCAL AUTHORITIES
10%

OTHER INCOME
14%

Festival Theatre
PITLOCHRY

Evening 8-0
FRIDAY
SEPT. 3

V14

TO BE RETAINED

FESTIVAL THEATRE
PITLOCHRY   0796 2680

EVENING 8-0 p.m.
FRIDAY
SEPTEMBER **3**

V14

PLEASE EXAMINE DATE
The management reserves the right to refuse
admittance or the refund of any money paid for tickets.
Latecomers will not be admitted until
a convenient break in the programme
THIS PORTION TO BE GIVEN UP

Did you know that for most professional theatre productions, musical events and other performances, the price of your ticket covers less than half the cost that has to be met?

Audiences share in helping to pay for performances at Pitlochry Festival Theatre.

But others need to share in covering the costs as well.

The Scottish Arts Council and the local authorities also help keep this theatre open and maintain the work that goes on in it.

Using a tiny proportion of taxes and rates, these bodies ensure that the ticket price you pay remains reasonable. They enable this theatre to give enjoyment to residents and tourists, and employment to many talented and skilled individuals.

The Scottish Arts Council assists more than 1,000 arts organisations, artists, performers and promoters throughout Scotland by providing financial support, advice and encouragement.

We all have a share in the arts in Scotland.

Scottish ▲rts Council

This page from a Pitlochry Festival Theatre programme illustrates in an appropriately dramatic way, the sources of a theatre's income. More of this kind of well-presented information would help audiences to understand arts funding.

ences assume that the theatre cannot be much good if nobody goes. Grant giving bodies are likely to agree with them. Theatre going is a shared experience — sharing with a lot of empty seats can reduce feelings of audience satisfaction. And audience response. And actor's morale. And therefore performance quality. And therefore seat sales. It can be a frightening downward spiral.

The number one requirement of box office success must be the quality of the productions staged. To believe otherwise would surely be to adopt a degree of cynicism incompatible with a positive role in theatrical activity. However, quality of product is not enough: high levels of seat occupancy are very dependent on success in bringing the merits of a particular production to the attention of its potential audience — a subject dealt with in chapter 9.

Pricing is critical. Theatre seat prices are rarely related to manufacturing costs. That would make seats too expensive and consequently empty. They tend therefore to be sold at the highest price that the market will bear. However with theatre seen as a social amenity, there is an obligation — certainly a moral one, if not always a statutory one — for any theatre supported by public funds to price at least a proportion of its seats at a level which makes them available to the full width of the population whether employed or not.

Rather than increase tickets in proportion with inflation, there is a tendency to try to hold prices in an effort to hold audiences. With theatre-going such a marginal activity for all but a tiny majority of the population, this is an almost inevitable reaction for a selling operation in a free market. However there is a cumulative effect in that seat prices have increasingly fallen behind the inflation adjusted equivalents of a few years ago. The peripherals of a night out at the theatre — transport, meals, etc, — have increased more than the ticket itself.

If seat prices are to be related to what the audience will pay rather than what the production actually cost, then the pricing will be flexible from one production to another. But how to determine what the price is? Well, there is analysis of past results for similar attractions. And analysis of the extent of the publicity that is likely to be generated. Audience research both formal and informal. And in theatre there always has to be a certain amount of reliance on hunches! As discussed in chapter 10, all is not lost if the pricing has gone wrong for there are methods of varying the price in response to careful monitoring of the progress of the box office sales operation.

If budgets are prepared on an assumption of 70 to 75% of capacity then any extra is pure 'bunce' — extra income which costs nothing to generate. It should be noted however that there can be a considerable difference between capacity percentages when expressed in financial or seating terms. Factors affecting this complex relationship between number of seats sold and amount of money taken include the varying effects of party reductions, subscriptions, special offers, etc. And some productions sell a high proportion of seats in the more expensive parts of the house; and vice versa. However when viewed over a year rather than a single week, these differentials tend to balance out sufficiently to get a reasonably stable financial figure for the 70 to 75% capacity that justifies a theatre's existence.

Catering

Catering is a recent growth area arising from the development of two new concepts about the purpose of a theatre building. Firstly the idea of a theatre visit being a complete night out, and secondly the growth in the practice of trying to keep a theatre building alive throughout the day.

Traditionally a theatre did not come to life until about half an hour before curtain up. Therefore catering could be limited to an interval bar with the usherettes selling chocolate boxes before the show and ice creams at the interval. That quaint institution, the matinée tea, could be served by passing pre-booked trays along the seating rows. Bars were open before the show but lightly patronised: the rush was at the interval. And there was no question of keeping open afterwards: from the fall of the curtain the entire staff became dedicated to lights out and lock up, with what frequently seemed to be an indecent haste.

This type of catering is reflected in the minimal front of house accommodation provided in many of the older theatres (with some notable exceptions such as the London Coliseum, designed with all day catering in mind). When older theatres are refurbished it is often possible to improve their facilities by extensions (as at Nottingham Royal), incorporation of adjacent premises (as at Bristol Royal) or by reorganising existing space (as at Norwich Royal).

Catering falls into four identifiable categories:

* **Performance catering**   Bars, coffee counters, sweets and ice-creams. Active from about half an hour before the performance until about half an hour after, although many theatres still close down after the last interval.
* **Pre-show catering**   Meals for ticket holders as part of the night-out concept.
* **All-day catering**   Bar service and meals open to the public throughout the day, with the bars operating as a pub during normal licensing hours.
* **Actor & staff catering**   Possibly a separate backstage canteen, but more usual to encourage sharing of audience facilities by offering discounts. Good discounts are an essential part of human staff relations . . . and, anyway, the public like to rub shoulders with the stars (and, remember, the leads of a regional rep are stars in their own regions).

All day catering may not be possible. There may not be space or, worse, the theatre may just not be situated in a street where it will attract trade. But a theatre that is alive all day is much more attractive than one which comes to life only when the rest of the town goes quiet. And many more people see the publicity and pass the box office window if they are in the habit of popping in for coffee or lunch.

The basic option is whether to manage the catering operation 'in house', or to contract it out to a concessionaire.

Sweets and ice cream can be conveniently run by the theatre since sales are largely in the hands of the usherettes who are required to be present anyway as safety attendants under the terms of the theatre's licence. Moreover, as well as offering profit levels that are so high that they are almost embarrassing, ice cream is easy to sell, with manufacturers providing free refrigerators and easy ordering systems.

Bars and meals however require a separate staff and a specialist manager. A theatre bar is difficult and expensive to staff when sales are concentrated into frantic rush periods of 15 or 20 minutes. Catering's relationship to box office has already been noted and many theatres are faced with a very difficult decision when considering whether to risk going for maximum potential profit with an in-house operation, or let a concessionaire take the risk with consequentially less profit potential for the theatre (although the theatre can share in success to some extent through a percentage deal). A concessionaire absorbs the hassle of staffing and ordering but the theatre loses control of the quality of service offered to the audience — a very important factor in the theatre's total image.

The decision can only be an individual one taken in terms of size, facilities, location and potential turnover.

Programmes

The programme should be regarded primarily as a service to the audience. It is a source of information about the performance and its background, and to many of the audience it is a souvenir to be preserved.

A programmme is a useful place for a theatre to promote its forthcoming productions and to give details of its box office procedures, supporters clubs, catering and other ancillary activities.

There are also certain contractual obligations to be fulfilled regarding programme billing, including biographies, for actors and production team. And its credits section can lubricate the ease with which firms either donate or discount their products for stage use.

Ideally such a programme should be free as it is in New York where the *Playbill* organisation is able to generate sufficient advertising to make free programmes available in all Broadway theatres. Indeed the practice of free programmes is common throughout North America.

European audiences are accustomed to paying for their programmes although there is a general feeling that the image of the theatre generally would benefit from the programme being included with the seat charge. Many of the programmes in the major theatres of Europe are relatively free from advertising and have comprehensive illustrated articles on the history and present concept of the work being performed. The major opera, dance and drama companies in Britain are moving towards this approach and the results can be rather impressive. This is the most desirable type of programme, although with short runs or with repertoire seasons the sales proceeds may have to be regarded as a contribution towards defraying publishing costs rather than as a source of potential profit.

Theatres have the alternative options of publishing their own programmes or using the services of an advertising contractor. The amount of work involved in an in-house programme advertising operation should not be underestimated: both selling space and getting invoices paid can be very time consuming. An agency undertakes to edit, print and deliver the programme at an agreed cost per thousand. Because this cost reflects the income that the agency receives from the advertisers, the theatre can afford to sell the programmes with sufficient margin to produce a useful addition to income. However programme income, like everything else, is related to good box office. The profit depends on a fairly accurate estimate of the number of programmes that will be required. It is always advisable to overestimate a little: if programmes run out, audiences get justifiably annoyed.

It is the agency's responsibility to seek, negotiate and bill the advertising: the theatre's only responsibility is to deliver by the agreed date to the printer, the 'copy' for the agreed number of theatre pages. Charges are kept competitive by such devices as printing several weeks' supply of coloured covers at one time, using standing type for the biographies of touring casts, and filling gaps in local advertising with national ads.

A large proportion of theatres outside London use the services of Stillwell Darby Ltd. The only common feature of all their programmes is four pages of articles weekly changed on theatre topics. Each theatre has its own cover although this can be changed for different productions (at additional cost) if required.

Advertising

The traditional painted advertising drop curtains seem to have disappeared from our theatres: presumably this is due partly to scenic designers demanding use of the flying space, partly to the labour costs of painting the ads, and partly due to current aesthetics. Slides projected on the fire curtain are also

The departments dealing with theatres are those devoted to drama, dance, much less in evidence than a few years ago. Film is occasionally used and tapes also, although there is a general feeling that advertising should not intrude into the actual performance space. Rumour from a 'usually reliable source' has it that in a certain theatre the curtain fell on a moment of high operatic tragedy. There was that wonderful moment of silence just before the applause breaks. That night it never came because, a fraction of a second after the curtain hit the deck, a tape recording blasted through the theatre — *just one cornetto*!

Advertising on foyer walls can attract a captive interval audience and so theatres have the possibility of raising income in this way, either directly or through agencies offering adverts in 'tasteful frames'. Showcases for jewellery and similar products are also possible. Even mustard. The choice is an aesthetic one.

Sundry sales

Theatre books and postcards, record albums, and other theatre related items are a desirable audience service as well as a possible income source. Margins can be severely eroded by labour costs but this is often overcome by using volunteers from the theatre's supporters club.

Musical acts usually tour records, brochures, T-shirts, badges and other merchandise. The sales commission can produce quite substantial sums. There is no limit, other than space, to a theatre's potential commercial activities. The only question is how far to go. My own feeling, certainly when I attend theatre as audience, is that sales and advertising (other than programme advertising) should not extend beyond theatre related items.

5   Awarded income

Financial assistance falls into two categories: grants and guarantees. Grants are contributions of a predetermined amount which are not dependent on the financial outcome of the performances which they are intended to assist. Guarantees are contributions to cover the actual extent of any loss incurred up to a nominated limit.

The other major division is between revenue and project funding. Revenue funding is a contribution towards the general operating expenses, whereas project funding is earmarked for a specific production or a definite activity such as a marketing campaign.

Awarded funds originate from two type of sources corresponding broadly to the public and private sectors.

Income sources in the public sector

Arts Council of Great Britain

Central Government funding of the arts in Britain is channelled through the Arts Council of Great Britain by means of an annual grant. The Arts Council negotiate the size of this grant with the government through the Office of Arts and Libraries in the Department of Education and Science. The distribution of the grant amongst arts organisations is totally the responsibility of the Arts Council, an independent body with aims and con- stitution embodied in a Royal Charter. The members of the Council are appointed for a period not exceeding five years by the Secretary of State for Education and Science, after consultation with the Secretaries of State for Scotland and Wales. The Council is advised by a team of specialist profes- sional officers and by a series of specialist voluntary panels and committees. All council, panel and committee members serve in an individual capacity, not as representatives of particular interests or organisations.

The system is generally agreed to be fair and workable although from time to time some disquiet is voiced that there is no elected element. It would however be difficult, almost certainly impossible, to reconcile elections with the principles of individual service. So it is fair to say that the Arts Council is really something of a contradiction — a successful self-promulgating democracy!

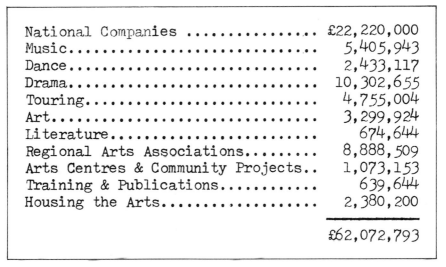

National Companies	£22,220,000
Music...........................	5,405,943
Dance...........................	2,433,117
Drama...........................	10,302,655
Touring.........................	4,755,004
Art.............................	3,299,924
Literature......................	674,644
Regional Arts Associations.......	8,888,509
Arts Centres & Community Projects..	1,073,153
Training & Publications..........	639,644
Housing the Arts................	2,380,200
	£62,072,793

Apportionment of Arts Council Grant (1981-82). contributions to the funding of building-based drama companies in 1981-82.

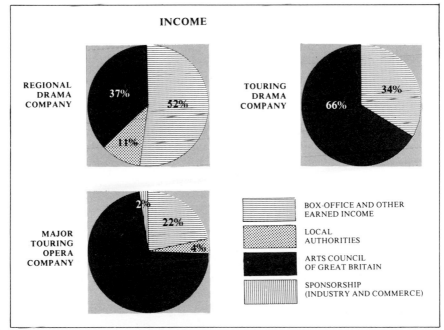

INCOME

REGIONAL DRAMA COMPANY   37%   52%   11%

TOURING DRAMA COMPANY   66%   34%

MAJOR TOURING OPERA COMPANY   2%   22%   4%

BOX-OFFICE AND OTHER EARNED INCOME

LOCAL AUTHORITIES

ARTS COUNCIL OF GREAT BRITAIN

SPONSORSHIP (INDUSTRY AND COMMERCE)

The required proportion of awarded income varies with the types and scope of theatre operation (ACGB Report, 1979-80).

music and touring. In general terms, these departments only support theatre *companies*, whether building based or touring. Theatres without their own companies are not accepted as clients by the Arts Council although the Council channels funds to Regional Arts Associations who assist theatres and arts centres housing mixed touring programmes. Arts Council funding is not normally available for amateur theatre.

The Touring Department has been playing an increasingly active role over the last decade in helping companies with the special costs involved in touring. In particular there has been a concern to ensure that the regions have an opportunity to see the work of the subsidised companies that because of size are inevitably based in London and other major metropolitan centres. Although this obviously applies primarily to the large-scale opera and ballet companies, recent policy has also been geared to making companies more readily available to smaller scale buildings, including arts centres, through regional touring grids.

The constitution, standards and policy of a theatre organisation must be acceptable to the Council before financial assistance can be offered. Organisations should be established as non-profit distributing bodies and preferably registered as charities. Applicants must submit detailed proposals for their programmes, supported by estimates. Once an organisation is in receipt of continuing subsidy, the Council appoints an assessor to evaluate its work and continuity of support is dependent on annual reassessment of a client's programmes and policy.

There are also various grants available for individual artists, and the schemes administered by the various departments are summarised in a comprehensive 'Guide to Awards and Schemes'.

Drama

Building-based companies

Basingstoke: Horseshoe Theatre Company Limited £	64,000
Birmingham Repertory Theatre Limited	360,000
Bolton: Octagon Theatre Trust Limited	100,000
Bristol Old Vic Trust Limited	370,000
Bromley: Churchill Theatre Trust Limited	77,750
Canterbury Theatre Trust Limited	4,381
Chester: Gateway Theatre Trust Limited	75,000
Colchester Mercury Theatre Limited	158,000
Coventry: Belgrade Theatre Trust (Coventry) Limited	180,000
Derby Playhouse Limited	141,000
Exeter: Northcott Devon Theatre and Arts Centre	173,000
Farnham Repertory Company Limited	113,000
Gloucestershire Everyman Theatre Company Limited	85,000
Guildford: Yvonne Arnaud Theatre Management Limited	92,000
Harrogate (White Rose) Theatre Trust Limited	110,000
Ipswich: Wolsey Theatre Company Limited	127,000
Lancaster: The Duke's Playhouse Limited	105,000
Leatherhead: Thorndike Theatre (Leatherhead) Limited	150,000

Arts Council contributions to the funding of building-based drama companies in 1981-82.

Leeds Theatre Trust Limited	200,000
Leicester Theatre Trust Limited	260,000
Liverpool: Merseyside Everyman Theatre Company Limited	146,250
Liverpool Repertory Theatre Limited	221,500
London: Alternative Theatre Company Limited	84,000
Caryl Jenner Productions Limited	180,500
English Stage Company Limited	430,425
Greenwich Theatre Limited	125,000
Half Moon Theatre Limited	85,200
Hampstead Theatre Limited	100,400
Hornchurch Theatre Trust Limited	131,000
Inter-Action Trust Limited	13,000
King's Head Theatre Productions Limited	37,000
Mermaid Theatre Trust Limited	150,000
National Youth Theatre of Great Britain	40,400
Oval House	44,000
Pioneer Theatres Limited	160,000
Soho Theatre Company Limited	45,000
Young Vic Company Limited	198,000
Manchester: Royal Exchange Theatre Company Limited	330,000
Manchester Young People's Theatre Limited	88,000
Newcastle: Tyne and Wear Theatre Trust Limited	175,000
Northampton Repertory Players Limited	80,000
Nottingham Theatre Trust Limited	358,000
Oldham Coliseum Theatre Limited	83,000
Oxford: Anvil Productions Limited	222,000
Plymouth Theatre Trust Limited	90,800
Richmond Fringe Limited	55,050
Salisbury Arts Theatre Limited	124,000
Scarborough Theatre Trust Limited	93,930
Sheffield: Crucible Theatre Trust Limited	365,000
Southend: Palace Theatre Trust (Southend-on-Sea) Limited	67,000
Stoke-on-Trent and North Staffordshire Theatre Trust Limited	140,000
Watford Civic Theatre Trust Limited	72,500
Worcester Arts Association (SAMA) Limited	70,000
Worthing and District Connaught Theatre Trust Limited	62,000
York Citizens' Theatre Trust Limited	158,500
	£7,771,586

Regional Arts Associations

Performance activities which are particularly regional in scope and char-
acter receive funding support from their Regional Arts Associations
(RAAs). This is in line with the Arts Council policy for regional development and with the regions' desire for local rather than central decision making. It is also seen as a method of involving local authorities in arts problems
so that they may be encouraged to undertake an increasing share of the
burden of funding the arts in the communities for whose total well-being
they are responsible, whether as elected members or officers.

There are a dozen arts associations in the English regions and further
three in Wales. The population distribution resulting from Scottish geography is not considered appropriate for regional decentralisation and RAA
functions are contained within the national role of the Scottish Arts Council
in Edinburgh.

Each of the independent RAAs has its own constitution and operational
structure. But allowing for the regional variations that would, almost by
definition, be expected, they are all in essence associations in which the
members are the county councils, district councils, arts organisations, and
concerned private individuals. Subscriptions of the participating local
authorities are scaled to the populations that they represent, although recent
financial climate has led to a number of authorities subscribing at a reduced
rate or withdrawing altogether. Faced with this, the associations have had
to devise a series of rather hair-splitting sanctions which try to balance pressure on under-participatory authorities with moral responsibilities towards
people living in these areas.

Indeed these responsibilities are to some extent formal as well as moral
because a considerable proportion of RAA funding is provided by the Arts
Council of Great Britain. The extent of this funding is such that any local
authority who does its sums diligently will usually discover that its ratepay-
ers get more out by grants than is payed in by subscription.

Regional associations have a major constitutional difference from the
central Arts Council in that their councils and/or management committees
have, in addition to nominated local authority representation, at least a
proportion of elected members. The staff of professional officers with expertise in their respective fields are advised by panels. These panels are rather
like local versions of the Arts Council panels in that they are specialists
serving as individuals. Also they tend to be self-perpetuating in that they
suggest their own new members, although such suggestions are normally
subject to confirmation by the controlling body of representative and elected
members. In general, because of the smaller scale of the operation, RAA
panels tend to have more of a decision making role than the Arts Council

Northern
Arts

Yorkshire
Arts
Association

North
West
Arts

Merseyside Arts
Trust

Lincolnshire
and Humberside
Arts

North Wales
Association
for the
Arts

East
Midlands
Arts

West
Midlands
Arts

Eastern Arts
Association

West Wales
Association
for the Arts

South-
East
Wales
Arts
Association

Southern
Arts
Association

South East
Arts

South West Arts

●Greater London
Arts Association

Regional Arts
Associations.

panels where expansion of scale has led inevitably to panels concentrating on policy advice rather than detailed decisions.

Grant application procedure is similar to that for Arts Council funding and involves submission of detailed financial proposals and subsequent accounts. Applicants are normally expected to be members of the Association although such membership does not confer any automatic right to assistance. First time applicants should submit a copy of their constitution and a statement describing policy, organisation and management.

The drama and dance panels of the RAAs have particular responsibility for theatre and this includes helping mixed programme theatres, arts centres, and all manner of smaller venues which accept touring productions.

Several RAAs support or reven maintain regional companies with a primary function of serving the dance and drama needs of their region. Opera is normally the responsibility of the music panels.

There have been some moves toward devolution of the support for regional building based companies from the central Arts Council to the RAAs. This devolution has been resisted on a number of grounds including fears that the RAAs may be more susceptible to political swings, and worries

Eastern Arts Association contributions to drama companies in 1981-82 for tours to specific venues in the Eastern region. In many cases these companies were also receiving Arts Council funding to assist with their annual costs (on a revenue basis) or specific production costs (on a project basis) while the venues were receiving general revenue assistance from Eastern Arts.

Touring — grants to theatre companies for tours

CAST — **Hotel Sunshine** in Cambridge, Norwich, Saffron Walden, Southend-on-Sea and Stowmarket	750
Cherub Theatre Company — **Macbeth** in Hemel Hempstead (2) Ipswich and King's Lynn (2)	400
C V One — **A Little Like Drowning** in Bedford, Cambridge and Leighton Buzzard	750
Eastern Angles — **Vital Statistics** in Butley and Ipswich (2)	100
Forkbeard Fantasy — **Seal of the Walrus** in Geldeston and Wetherden	160
Incubus — **The Revengers Comedy** in Beccles, Colchester (2), Garboldisham and Wetherden	800
Jill Freud and Company — **Canterbury Tales** in Billericay, Ely, Leighton Buzzard, Walberswick, Wells-next-the-Sea, Welwyn Garden City and Wisbech (3)	350
Major Road Theatre Company — **The Hype** in Basildon (2), Beccles, Bungay (2), Leiston and Luton	350
Medieval Players — **The Ship of Fools** in Bishop's Stortford (2), Ipswich (2), Saffron Walden and Ware (2)	750
Mikron Theatre Company — **Mud In Your Eye** and **I'd Go Back Tomorrow** in Apsley (2), Broxbourne, Hunton Bridge, Linslade and St Margarets (Hertfordshire)	158
Moving Parts — **Space Invaders** in Cambridge, Clacton, Costessey, Hitchin, Ipswich, Norwich, Ramsey, Stevenage and Thetford (£250) and **No Kidding** in Cambridge (2), Costessey, Diss, Hitchin, Letchworth (2), Norwich and Ramsey (£250)	500

that another administrative layer may syphon off a proportion of the available cash. For the moment it has been agreed that any devolution will only take place with the assent of the devolved theatre.

Local authorities

The impetus for today's universal involvement of local authorities in arts funding came from the Local Government Act of 1948 which authorised expenditure on the arts of a sum up to a maximum of the product of a sixpenny rate. Very few, if any, reached this maximum and arts allocations, both as a result of this act and the amending 1972 Act, have remained discretionary rather than mandatory. However there has been a continual growth, both in direct provision of theatre performances and in support for non-profit distributing theatre organisations. This is in addition to local authority funds channelled through Regional Arts Associations.

Mrs Worthington's Daughters — **Angels of War** in King's Lynn (2) and Lowestoft (3)	750
Paines Plough — **The Decameron** and **Days Here So Dark** in Bedford (2), Hemel Hempstead (2), Norwich (2) and Wells-next-the-Sea (2)	750
Perspectives Theatre Company — **Devil on the Heath** in Chatteris, Haddenham, Littleport, Northborough Peterborough (2), Ramsey, St Ives, Sawtry, Swavesey, Whittlesey and Wisbech (2) (£1,500) and **No Pasaran** in Cambridge, Luton, Peterborough, St Ives, Sawtry and Swavesey (£200)	1,700
7:84 Theatre Company — **Night Class** in Gt Yarmouth, Norwich and Southend (£300) and two further productions in Gt Yarmouth (£175)	475
Stirabout — for performances at prisons and borstals in Blundeston, Gaynes Hall, Hockley, Hollesley, Norwich and Stradishall	500
Theatre Machine — **The Best of Est** in Norwich, Colchester, and Hemel Hempstead	250
TNT — **Don't Look Back** in Cambridge (4), Hatfield (2), Hemel Hempstead (2) and Luton	400
TOOT — **Moving Stills** in Bradwell, Earsham, Lingwood, Sheringham (3) and Wells-next-the-Sea (2)	250
Wolsey Theatre-Go-Round — **Relatively Speaking** in Aldeburgh, Bressingham, Cockfield, Debenham, Felixstowe, Gt Cornard, Gt Yarmouth, Hitcham, Ipswich, Lowestoft, Martlesham, Rendham, Southwold, Stowmarket, Toppesfield, Wenhaston and Woodbridge	2,500
	12,543

There appears to be no national policy for local government involvement in the arts, and very little national guidance. The type of involvement varies according to local conditions and indeed this response to local need is just what, at least in theory, regional government should be about. The extent of the response does depend to quite a considerable extent on pressure from the arts lobby and, with arts as a minority if vocal interest in the community, it is hardly suprising that the arts seem to do rather better when the political doctrines are evenly balanced than when either side has a clear majority.

With recent curbs on public spending, the local authorities have not been in a position to develop their support which has consequently been restricted to maintaining existing clients at a level which not only allows nothing for growth but contains a less than adequate adjustment for inflation. There is an almost annual pattern of crisis when theatre grants inevitably appear on a list of possible cuts. However support is normally maintained provided that the theatre appears to be enjoying artistic, but more importantly, box office success. It should be noted that in these circumstances, success tends to be measured in attendance percentages rather than financial results.

Direct control of a theatre by an authority is more expensive for them than contributing to the support of a theatre run by a trust company. This is because the minimum standards of pay and conditions for council employees are considerably above the going rates in trust theatres where many people have to be prepared to accept a considerable element of job satisfaction in compensation for the level of financial remuneration available in the public sector or most branches of private industry.

Income sources in the private sector

Industrial sponsorship

The redistribution of wealth that has been a feature of society in recent years has virtually brought to an end the private patronage that formed an important role in arts funding for centuries. Part of this missing patronage has been taken over by the state, but the assistance of industry is being sought to assume an increasing proportion of the balance.

Although the volume of industrial sponsorship is on the increase, sponsors naturally tend to prefer to be associated with the more glamorous types of traditional theatre, particularly the nationally recognised opera, ballet, and drama companies. It is acknowledged that there is a danger that less attractive experimental work, as well as that of the more routine, less spectacular playhouses, might suffer through this inevitable bias in support. However every theatre should be able to get some sort of help from local industry if its case is presented properly.

It must be emphasised that the concept of sponsorship is currently very fashionable and every theatre organisation seeking a share in public funds should not only seek but should be seen to be seeking help from industry.

The Government's Office of Arts and Libraries have produced leaflets offering guidance to potential givers and receivers. These are not the usual soberly printed type of official civil service publication but have typography and layout appropriate to a sales operation.

The benefits of sponsorship are listed in this publication as:

*   Bringing the company name before the general public.
*   Bringing the company name before its own special market.
*   Promotion of a special product.
*   Improvement of an employee's and customer's way of life.
*   Tax relief.

And there is a valuable list, largely reproduced below, of how to go about getting sponsorship once a firm has been selected as a potential target for a positive scheme, remembering that firms like to be associated with a definite identifiable event rather than just a general operation:

*   Try to learn about your potential sponsors — their objectives, ambitions, financial position, who takes the decisions about public relations.
*   Allow time for companies to consider and discuss. Plan well ahead. Anticipation is the key.
*   Choose your moment properly. Find out about the company's financial year and when the details of the community or public relations are settled.
*   Try to avoid a cold approach — assume a human relationship — you are both part of the same community.
*   Find the right person in the organisation, write or telephone and ask for a meeting. Write personally, avoid stereotyped letters.
*   Be businesslike. You are also a professional, making your living at what you do and what you are good at.
*   Make it clear that you have a proposal which will be to their benefit.
*   Set out clearly and concisely:
    (a)   What it will cost.
    (b)   How you will achieve it.
    (c)   What you are prepared to offer.
    (d)   What you want from a sponsor.
*   Be confident — you are seeking a business deal between professionals.
*   Be flexible — be prepared to modify your plans to meet a sponsor's needs.

* Do not assume that anyone has a moral responsibility to give money.
* Do not be deterred by apparently hostile questions.
* Do not confuse artistic vision with wish fulfillment.
* Do not promise more than you can achieve.
* Do not be condescending towards someone who knows less about theatre than you do.
* Never give up!

ABSA

The Association for Business Sponsorship of the Arts (ABSA) is an association of business organisations which are involved in sponsorship of the arts. ABSA is a registered charity but is neither a fund raising nor a grant giving body. It will not seek sponsorship for arts events, but it does seek arts events for sponsors. It plays a major role in publicising the benefits of sponsorship and in disseminating information through advertising, publications, seminars, conferences, etc. ABSA organises seminars for arts administrators and provides a consulting service for arts organisations seeking sponsors.

Lotteries

In many parts of the world, lotteries have been a major source of theatrical funding, particularly for building new theatres. In Britain they did not become legal until the Lotteries and Amusements Act of 1976. This produced an initial surge of activity but the momentum has not been maintained, possibly because there was such a rash of small lotteries everywhere. However several theatres have made useful gains. The Norwich City Lottery, run in association with the Theatre Royal and utilising that theatre's particularly effective publicity machine, has made some £218,000 available to the theatre in the years 1977-1982, being 60% of the proceeds.

Supporters' organisations

Whatever they are called (Friends of the Theatre, Theatre Club, Playgoers Society, etc.) supporting organisations fall into two categories. Some are directly managed by the theatre, rather in the nature of a marketing device offering priority bookings, discounts, special offers etc. in return for an annual subscription. The majority are autonomous bodies with an independent constitution and elected office bearers. Their purpose is to promote the theatre in its community by forming a body of opinion which is broadly sympathetic to their theatre's aims, plus providing support both as the nucleus of a regular audience and by supplying practical and/or financial help. Such organisations are normally members of the national 'Federation of Playgoers Societies'.

Some clubs make an annual contribution to their theatre's revenue, intended primarily to defray the cost of servicing their members with mailings. However supporter's clubs, like all funding bodies, rather prefer to contribute to identifiable causes and often undertake special fundraising activities of the traditional kind (coffee mornings, auctions, bazaars etc.) to raise money for such purposes. As well as direct financial aid, they can often supply money-saving practical assistance. For example, the committee of the Friends of the Theatre Royal at Bury St Edmunds, having raised funds to supply and lay new carpeting, arrived one night at the fall of the curtain armed with screwdrivers to remove the seats. Next evening they returned to replace them on the new carpet.

Modes of awarding funds

There is currently a considerable degree of flexibility in whether awarded income is made available in the form of grants or guarantees. Which of these modes carries most incentive for maximum effort on the part of the receiving organisation is a matter for some conjecture. It takes little expertise in creative accountancy for an organisation to ensure that it is able to call upon the full amount of a guarantee. On the other hand, administrators with a sensitive response to the attitudes of particular funding bodies may from time to time contrive to require less than the full guarantee in order to create an impression of efficiency which may lead to a sympathetic climate for consideration of future applications.

However there does seem to be a current trend towards project rather than revenue awards: this is a simple matter of the cash dispensers seeking to exert more control over how their funds are used, in both administrative and artistic terms. Certainly any new theatre company seeking funds is more likely to get a series of project grants, with graduation to annual revenue funding only following after a demonstration of stability — again both in administrative and artistic terms.

Income proportions

Most theatre organisations receive income from most of the sources described, although the proportion varies according to the type of organisation. In particular, the proportion contributed by box office will vary a great deal between types of theatre with different production costs.

Within the subsidised area, the Arts Council and the Regional Arts Associations are continually re-drafting the lines of demarcation. For some years, the broad split has been between building based companies looking to ACGB and mixed programme theatres to the RAAs, theatre companies being a shared responsibility between ACGB and RAAs depending on their national or regional role. However there does seem now to be an increasing, if gradual, move towards devolution.

From time to time the various funding sources try to stimulate each other's contributions by making 'pound for pound' offers or even conditions for grant award. This type of ploy is used particularly to encourage generosity in local authorities, although Britain is still a long way from the Central European situation where theatres are universally regarded as a matter of civic responsibility, indeed of civic pride.

6 Expenditure and budgeting

Survival is dependent upon a fine balance between expenditure and income. Expenditure can be controlled, even quite rigidly controlled. But income, especially earned income, is subject to a degree of variation that can reach quite alarming proportions. A major task of any theatre's administration is to budget realistically and then monitor actual results against estimates. This monitoring must be accurate and up to date.

Overhead expenditure

Expenditure falls into two categories: overheads and programme costs. A theatre operation has certain fixed costs. In the case of a production company operating without a theatre base these will be quite simple and small. Office rent, rates, heat and light. Salaries for a small permanent staff (say producer, business manager, production manager, secretary). Plus admin expenses like stationery, postage, telephone, entertaining, travelling and membership of management associations.

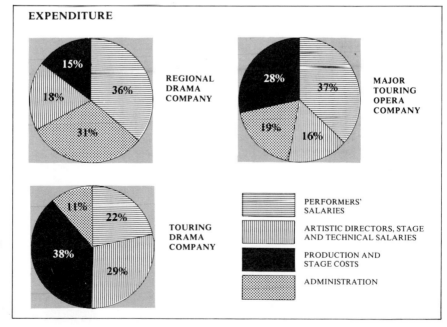

The proportion of expenditure in various categories will vary with the type and scope of theatre operation (ACGB annual report, 1978-80).

For a theatre building the overheads can be very substantial before a single performance ever graces the stage. These costs may be summarised as:

* Building expenditure, including rent (or interest charges), rates, water, oil and electricity, cleaning, repairs and maintenance.

* Administrative expenditure, including salaries and wages, fees and subscriptions, stationery, postage, telephones, travel, accountancy and audit.

* Publicity expenditure, including advertising, posters, leaflets, diaries and entertaining.

* Stage expenditure, including materials and equipment for general stage maintenance, not allocatable to specific productions.

* Contingency reserve

To monitor expenditure, up to date 'actuals' (i.e. figures of expenditure) must always be available for comparison with the budget. For each item the essential figures are:

* Annual budget
* Budget to date
* Actual to date
* Variance + or −

Most average size theatres can risk monitoring formally on a monthly basis, only the biggest need do it weekly. But no theatre is small enough to risk quarterly analysis. The 'budget to date' figure can be derived by a simple division of the annual figure into equal amounts, or the total figure can be apportioned to take account of anticipated fluctuations in payments over the year.

Formulation of next year's budget for overheads is carried out by projecting ahead from this comparison of current budget and current actuals. For each item the appropriate figures are:

* This year's budget
* This year's actual to date
* This year's estimated final actual
* Next year's base
* Next year's budget

The 'estimated final actuals' can be projected from the current year's variance with budget, taking into consideration any forseeable changes before the year end. The base figure for the next year is the figure at a determined date, usually about six months prior to the next financial year,

EAST LOAMSHIRE STRUGGLING THEATRE TRUST LTD.

Gate Theatre Overhead Budget

31:10:82.

	81-82 Budget	81-82 Actuals (to date)	81-82 Actuals (Final, projected)	82-83 Base	82-83 Budget
Buildings					
Rent	1,000	500	1,000	1,100	1,100
Rates	500	274	547	550	600
Insurance	700	600	720	700	800
Water rates	450	212	423	450	500
Oil	900	300	850	900	1,000
Electricity	5,500	2,765	5,900	6,000	7,000
Cleaning	1,000	430	1,000	1,000	1,100
Repairs & Maint.	2,500	1,200	2,200	2,500	2,500
	12,610	6,281	12,640	13,200	14,600
Administration					
Salaries & wages	42,000	24,960	44,500	46,000	50,000
Fees & Subs.	800	550	800	800	900
Stationery	950	453	900	950	1,000
Postage	2,350	1,265	2,500	2,650	3,000
Telephones	1,600	991	1,700	1,700	2,000
Travelling	400	195	370	400	500
Tickets	1,200	952	1,200	1,200	1,500
Accountancy & audit	800	650	800	800	900
	50,100	30,016	52,770	54,500	59,800
Stage					
Consumables	2,700	1,474	2,500	3,000	3,000
Hires	900	520	950	1,000	1,000
	3,600	1,994	3,450	4,000	4,000
Publicity					
Advertsising	8,200	4,350	8,500	9,000	10,000
Printing	2,100	1,560	2,200	2,500	2,800
Photography	300	170	250	300	350
Entertaining	300	187	320	350	350
	10,900	6,267	11,270	12,150	13,500
TOTALS	77,210	44,558	80,130	83,850	91,900
+ Contingency	4,000	4,000	4,000	5,000	5,000
	81,210	48,558	84,130	88,850	96,900

Expenditure budget for a small mixed programme theatre's overheads.

when grant awarding bodies are preparing their budgets and require estimates from their clients. This base figure is determined from the estimated final actuals for the current year by taking into account any changes of policy or known changes in costs for the next year. The actual budget figure is derived firstly by the addition of a notional inflationary figure to the base. As the new financial year approaches, this budget figure can be gradually refined as the actual level of inflationary increase in each category becomes known.

Programme costs

Programme costings split into two rather clearly defined parts: production costs and running costs. The production budget covers all the expenditure on salaries and materials up to the point immediately before the first public performance. Thereafter the running costs are the weekly sum to cover all performance expenditure.

Production costs

Typical production costs include:

*	Physical Production	Scenery building and painting
		Furniture and set dressings
		Properties
		Costumes
*	Fees	Management
		Director
		(Choreographer)
		Designer
		Lighting designer
		(Sound designer)
*	Advertising and Publicity	Press agent
		Newspaper advertising
		Printing and artwork
		(Signwriting)
		Photography
		Press releases, conferences, etc.
*	Rehearsal expenses	Salaries
		National Insurance
		Rehearsal rooms
		Transport
*	Miscellaneous	Scripts
		Get-in to theatre

The production manager is responsible for budgeting and scheduling the preparation of scenery, costumes, properties, lighting and sound. A provisional sum for this is included in the total budget but modification may be required at the point known as 'model approval' when the designs are approved by the director prior to going to the workshops. At this point a reduction in scenic requirements or an increase in budget may be necessary. Or more likely both: compromise is a basic technique of theatre manufacture.

Budgets for fees, formulated by the administrator in consultation with the director must take account of union agreements and these are outlined in later chapters, as are the items to be budgeted for publicity and advertising.

Running costs

If the run is of a pre-determined length, the total production costs can be divided by the number of weeks to ascertain the weekly rate at which production costs should be amortised. This figure plus the weekly running costs gives the total weekly sum required for the production to break even.

It can however be difficult to calculate a fixed figure for the running costs because some of the payments are based on a sliding scale related to box office returns.

The following may be subject to percentages:

* Star actors
* Authors
* Director
* Designers
* Miscellaneous royalties such as Performing Right Society etc.

But the following are normally fixed:

* Non-star actors
* Stage management
* National Insurance
* Equipment hire charges
* Advertising and printing
* Press agent
* Management fee
* Stage management accounts
* Wardrobe expenses

For a theatre company renting a West End theatre there will be additional weekly running costs of theatre rental (related to box office results) and a more or less regular level of contra account for all the theatre staff and services that are provided by the theatre but are the responsibility of the renting producer. The company will be responsible for all advertising and this will consequentially be a high item.

For a touring play there will be no rent and the theatre contra will be relatively small with only some staff overtime and miscellaneous items to be paid for. Advertising costs will be limited to a share of special display advertising. However there will be the weekly costs of get-outs, scenery transport, plus company transport and subsistence allowances. The weekly break-even cost of a tour (weekly running plus amortisation of production) indicates the minimum sum that is required as the touring company's share of the box office receipts — and therefore the sum to be sought as guarantee. A subsidised touring company may be able to write the production costs off against awarded income and it may also be able to do so with a proportion of the weekly costs. Indeed if it is a music, dance or large scale drama theatre company, this will be the only viable possibility.

Depending on its budgeted income, a mixed programme theatre may require to take a predetermined average figure from its box office share as a contribution to overheads. Many MPTs and arts centres however aim to cover their overheads from awarded income and miscellaneous earned income, leaving all box office receipts to pay for the programme. As costs rise and venues try to improve programme quality, the box office becomes insufficient to meet direct programme costs and this area too needs a subsidy.

Where a theatre produces its own programme, the division between overheads and production costs becomes indistinct since many personnel overlap. However it is still useful thinking to try to separate the two. Producing theatres inevitably need considerable subsidy since the short runs offer very little time to amortise production costs. In the case of lyric and drama theatres with large casts, musicians and staff, both the running and production costs are well beyond a level that could be recouped from the box office without raising seat prices beyond a socially acceptable level.

Income budgeting

Earned income is difficult to predict because it is dependent on box office success. Variations in seat sales affect not only ticket income but also receipts from all other activities such as bars and programmes which are related to audience numbers. High quality productions combined with marketing expertise can level out these variations. But theatre success is continually subject to winds of fashion that defy analysis: the good show, brilliantly publicised, that resolutely refuses to take off at the box office, and the ill-mounted pot boiler, ineptly sold, that pulls them in. Earned income budg-

```
            BUDGET FOR SMALL MODERN ONE-SET PLAY TOUR (1981)


 PRODUCTION COSTS                         WEEKLY RUNNING COSTS

 Physical Production                      Star One................ £400
                                          Star Two................  350
 Settings.................... £3000       3 cast @ 110 ...........  330
 Costumes....................  1000       CM/SM...................  150
 Furniture & Props...........  1000       DSM.....................  105
                                          2 x ASMs @ 80 ..........  160
                                          Wardrobe  ..............   80
 Pre-Rehearsal Expenses                   NHI (@ 13%) ............  200
                                          Touring allowances .....  300
 CM/SM (as Production Manager)  300       Holiday pay reserve.....  100
 NHI (@ 13%)................    40         Company travel .........  120
 Director (Preparation).......  500       Set travel .............  350
 Designer....................   500       Booking expenses/fees....  75
 Audition Expenses...........   250       Printing................  300
 Graphics & Publicity........   500       Royalties...............  400
                                          Hire charges............   50
 Rehearsal Expenses (3 weeks)             Theatre contra..........  200
                                          Get-out & gratuities.....  100
 Director....................   800       SM a/c..................   50
 CM/SM.......................   450       Wardrobe a/c............   40
 DSM.........................   315       Insurances..............   50
 2 x ASM @ 80 ...............   480       Management Fee .........  200
 Wardrobe (2 wks @ 80).......   160       Accountancy.............   30
 Understudy obligations......    90       Contingency.............  100
 NHI (@ 13%) ................   340                                 ————
 Rehearsal rooms.............   200                                 £4240
 SM accounts ................   200
 Scenery transport...........   350       plus amortisation of
 Get-out from workshops......   100       production costs.......   782
 Vans for collections etc....   100
 Photography & prints .......   100       TOTAL WEEKLY COSTS..... £5022.
 Press Material..............   100                               ———————
 Management fees.............   600
 Accountancy.................    30       Which  suggests that an average
 Contingency.................  1000       weekly guarantee of £5,000 from
                                          each theatre should be sought by
                               ———————    the touring company.
                               £12505

 Amortised over 16 weeks  =  £782 weekly.
```

Example of budget for a simple one-set modern dress touring play.

eting is probably at its easiest in a regional production theatre with a regular audience built up by a mixture of dependable standards plus series bookings. Income budgeting is certainly at its most difficult in the West End where the main ingredients are inevitably hope founded on faith.

Grants and guarantees are a more stable source of income but budgeting the level of such awarded income is not easy. For one thing, they are rarely confirmed very far in advance. There are submissions, discussions, assessments, recommendations, rumours, threats and crises on which to construct a hopefully accurate guess: but the level of subsidy awarded tends to be confirmed after the deadline for making assumptions based on that level.

In an ideal world, the subsidy level awarded would be the projected shortfall between earned income and the actual costs based on a reasonable standard of presentation coupled with proper salaries and working conditions for the performing, production and administrative staffs. Unfortunately this is rarely even remotely possible in the current and foreseeable climate. At best, the level of awarded income is based on a less than adequate inflation adjustment to last year's figure. There is therefore a continual squeeze upon costs with the maintenance of standards dependent upon the continuing goodwill of personnel.

Principal income categories for budgeting are:

EARNED
* Box office receipts
* Bars and catering
* Programmes and miscellaneous sales
* (Rentals of sets, costumes, etc)
* (Residual royalties from production transfers etc)
* (Bank interest, investment income etc)

AWARDED
* Arts Council +/or Regional Arts Associations.
* Sponsors
* Donations

Budget balancing

It will be obvious from the foregoing that balancing a theatre budget is not a process that can be carried through entirely on scientific principles based only on logical decisions. Having checked and re-checked all the calculations, theatre administrators need ultimately to have faith in their entrepreneurial instincts for estimating income; and in their intuitive ability for analysing the hints, rumours, leaks and unconfirmed promises that precede the formal offers of assistance from the funding establishment. Financial planning decisions which should be sequential must be taken simultaneously. Faith, hope and strong nerves must back up the entrepreneurial instinct to such an extent that the only measure of administrative ability would seem to be a record of survival.

Award applications

The budget figures provide the basis for all applications for grants and guarantees. Several organisations, particularly the Arts Council and some Regional Arts Associations have a prescribed form for setting out figures either on a pro-forma or plain paper. The figures need to be supported by other information and most grant awarding organisations issue guidelines to assist clients in the preparation of their submissions. The following points, however, are universal to most application methods:

* Discuss your proposals informally with the appropriate officer before making a written submission.

* Submit applications in a format suitable for photocopying, i.e. always send the original, typed in black on white A4 paper, putting the company's name and date at the top of each sheet, and try to restrict to less than six sheets.

* Describe the constitution, aims and objectives of the company with details of personnel, casting, etc.

* Describe past and projected programmes, particularly performances planned during the period covered by the application.

* Give financial results of past and current seasons. This can be in abbreviated summary form if accounts are being regularly submitted because you are a regular client.

* Give estimated expenditure and income as budgeted. Do not calculate wages at less than appropriate union rate and always include National Insurance contributions. Do not estimate author's royalties at less than 7½% of gross box office receipts.

* Include any other anticipated subsidy (including other applications) in the income total. The difference between income and expenditure is the subsidy requested.

7   Contracting people

We have already noted the two basic options for any theatre building: to present productions of its own manufacture, or productions supplied by an independent manufacturing company. Whichever method is used, there are certain common procedures. Most differences arise from whether personnel are engaged for a one-off or for a season.

The starting point is the producer who packages the show by bringing together script, director, possibly star(s) and the money. The producer's function is seen at its purest and simplest in the West End where it requires the single-minded determination of an individual to make a show happen. A West End production organisation can be surprisingly small, perhaps just the producer supported by a business manager, production manager and secretary. All other functions are subcontracted to the individual or organisation most appropriate for the requirements of a particular production.

National or regional theatres producing their own show 'in house' do not use the term producer although the producer's function is carried out by whoever bears the responsibility, although not neccessarily the title, of artistic director. Whereas a producer can be autocratic in decision an artistic director is increasingly encouraged, even forced, to be the leader in a corporate process. This is an inevitable consequence of the shift of financing from the private individual to the public purse. Corporate decisions should be better but they are certainly slower: one has to hope that the first will compensate for the latter.

In such production companies, the administrator plays a major role in the corporate decisions. Indeed it is increasingly the administrator who reports on financial matters directly to the Board, rather than through the artistic director. The sharing of responsibility varies from theatre to theatre and can be a source of tension between administration, artistic direction and board members. I myself am convinced that the ultimate responsibility for all aspects of a theatre operation must lie in the hands of one person given virtual dictatorial powers which, through force of personality, are rarely required to be exercised. Such a person must surely be the artistic leader although one whose talents are accompanied by a sense of financial responsibility.

The producer/artistic director selects a director appropriate for the script. It is then that director's responsibility to choose a production team of designers for set, costumes, props, lighting and sound, a stage management team and an acting cast. Although selection is the director's responsibility, the producer will want to be involved in at least approval of the team. For a 'one-off' production the team can be assembled from the most appropriate specialists available in the freelance pool. For an 'in house' production, choice will be limited to the theatre's contracted permanent or seasonal team.

Once actors and production team have agreed in principle to take part, their contracts have to be negotiated by the administration. In most cases the minimum terms and working conditions are the subject of agreements between the unions and management associations.

Management associations

Society of West End Theatre

For some eighty years, SWET has been the trade association through which the West End theatre owners and producers negotiate with the unions and other organisations. Membership is around the eighty mark with the Society representing some forty-five West End theatres and most established producers. In addition to its dealings with outside bodies, the Society provides an internal forum for the producers and theatre owners to discuss their common interests and landlord/tenant relationships. The Society however has no standard contract or formal guidelines for agreements between its producing manager and theatre owning members. Recently SWET has taken on a wider function of publicity and marketing and in 1979 appointed a Development Officer to seek ways of promoting the image of the West End theatre as a whole.

Theatrical Management Association

The TMA is the trade association of the theatrical managers who operate in theatres other than the West End group covered by SWET. This association includes both producing and theatre operating members. Today's TMA was formed in the late 1970s by merger of the two established commercial management organisations, the original Theatrical Management Association of 1894 and the Association of Touring and Producing Managers (ATPM) with the Council of Regional Theatre (CORT). CORT had originally been formed in 1944 as the Council of Repertory Theatres to provide a forum and representative body for the growing subsidised sector. The amalgamation of all three bodies into TMA was partly a recognition that there is only one kind of theatre operation and that it requires subsidy in one form or another. Membership is open to individuals, local authorities, trusts or companies concerned either with the management of theatres or similar places of public entertainment in the regions, or with the production of theatrical events or other recognised forms of live entertainment for presentation in such venues. Applications are considered by a committee, with the full membership given an opportunity to object to any particular applicant. After a probationery period, members normally graduate to full membership which, for producing managers, carries the very useful cash-flow perk of exemption from the requirement to deposit a salary bond with the Provincial Theatre Council for each production.

Independent Theatre Council

The ITC was formed in 1976 as a management association for groups and individuals working in alternative theatre. It aims to represent its members' interests in negotiations with unions and funding bodies.

Theatres National Committee

SWET and TMA are independent bodies although they share offices and secretariat. Their joint interests are looked after by the TNC which also includes the Association of Circus Proprietors of Great Britain. The TNC deals with matters which affect theatres on a national basis including union agreements for areas such as opera and ballet which affect both SWET and TMA. The TNC also makes representations on behalf of its constituent members to the Government, Arts Council and other public bodies.

Unions

Equity

British Actors Equity Association in fact represents actors, stage managers, directors and designers. It is unique in that it is a trade union with the majority of its members out of work at any given time. Despite this, and a degree of internal dissent that reflects the individualism of the actor's art, Equity has in recent years made enormous strides in improving the working conditions of its members. Since actors' reputations have such an important effect upon box office income there has always been, and will continue to be, considerable imbalance between the stars and the rest. More realistic minimum salaries now ensure reasonable rewards for those at the beginning of their careers: both union and management acknowledge that it is the experienced non-name actors whose skills are purchased at unrealistically low rates which neither relate logically to the extremes of their own profession nor bear fair comparison with salaries outside the theatre. Thus much of the current and future negotiation is likely to be concentrated on what is known as MRSL (Middle Range Salary Levels) which, unlike minima, are very complex to negotiate.

NATTKE

The National Association of Theatrical, Television and Kine Employees is the oldest established trade union in the entertainment industry. It represents the interest of all backstage technicians and most front of house employees including box office staff. NATTKE is also the union representing many skills in workshops whether located in theatres or belonging to outside contractors servicing the theatre industry.

Theatre Writers Union, and Writers' Guild of Great Britain

Dramatists have only recently started to seek standard agreements with the management associations. They are represented by the Theatre Writers Union and the Writers' Guild of Great Britain who are negotiating jointly on behalf of their members.

Agreements

Relations between managers and artists in the West End are regulated by the London Theatre Council whose membership comprises nominees of the Society of West End Theatre and Equity. This council supervises the adoption of standard contracts and the settlement of any disputes arising. It has authority to require managers to deposit an appropriate sum as a condition of registration. The amount of this deposit is normally the artists' salaries for two weeks. Members of SWET are normally indemnified by their Society and thus exempt from the requirements of depositing.

The Provincial Theatre Council performs the same function for regional theatre, with TMA and Equity as the members. A deposit is normally required from managers who are not members of TMA.

Each union negotiates a series of agreements with SWET for the West End and TMA for the regions, and some of these are discussed below. In addition there are a number of house agreements which take account of the special circumstances of certain theatres, particularly the major repertoire companies.

Actors' contracts, London West End

The West End is governed by the Equity/SWET agreement which establishes provisions for:
* Minimum salaries negotiable annually.

* Holiday pay.
* Illness payments.
* Overtime payments.
* Understudy provisions and payments
* Travel for out of London openings
* Clarification of matters such as costumes, make-up, hairdressers, scripts, publicity material, billing, photographs, insurance, prosecutions, discrimination etc.

The details of the provisions are listed in a schedule of some twenty small printed A4 pages which define and supplement the twelve summarising clauses of the Standard Contract and are held to form an integral part of it. This contract is signed by manager and artist, with a copy filed at Equity.

SWET have a casting agreement whereby they will not offer engagements to artists unless they are full members of Equity (a full member being one who has completed forty weeks of provisional membership). The agreement includes provision for a manager to apply to Equity for a waiver if there is a specific casting problem. And this, like all provisions in the contract is subject to final arbitration by the London Theatre Council.

Opera and ballet

Agreements for opera and ballet have been negotiated between Equity and the Theatres National Committee: consequently they are jointly approved by both the London and Provincial Theatre Councils. These contracts reflect the special nature of working practices in opera and ballet respectively: in most cases they form the basis of individual house agreements made with the major opera and ballet companies.

The basic opera agreements are for salaried singers, for guest artists and for stage management. The opera world still uses the old title 'producer' for the functions carried out by the director in other forms of theatre: there are standard contracts for both staff producers and for those engaged for a single production. Special provisions include procedures and fees for the revivals that are an inherent part of the repertoire and stagione systems that form the basis of an opera house's operation. The producer is also given residual rights in the creative elements of production when that production is either sold or licensed.

Ballet contracts include specific provision for the 'class' that is an essential part of the dancer's daily routine. There is a very specific clause about providing adequate working conditions including a requirement that temperature be maintained at not less than 65 degrees Fahrenheit. There is a requirement that the artist shall join the Dancers' Pension Scheme. And a surprisingly stern clause entitled 'Conduct Unbecoming', although dancers could surely be regarded as possibly the least intemperate members of the theatre community.

Regional theatre

Performers in regional theatres are covered by two Equity/TMA agreements — one for commercial tours and seasons including non-subsidised repertory, and one for subsidised repertory and repertoire.

Provincial commercial agreement

Much of the schedule deals with matters similar to those listed above for the West End, but there is some shift of emphasis, and some added provisions reflecting the particular conditions of touring such as:

* Subsistence and touring allowances.
* Transport.
* Weeks out (i.e. non-performing weeks during a tour).

In many provisions, particularly salaries and the working week of forty-eight hours, the performers' terms are less favourable than in the West End contract. However holiday entitlement is better and there is a shorter qualifying period.

This agreement has standard specialised contract forms to cover:

* Non-subsidised repertory at provincial theatres.
* Resident seasons in provincial theatres.
* Sessional work for tours or seasons in the provinces (e.g. children's theatres, studios, workshops etc)
* Provincial theatre tours.

There are two Equity/TMA casting agreements applicable to contracts within this provincial commercial area. The first applies to tours and seasons and makes the casting of Equity members mandatory. In the case of 'number ones' (a traditional nomenclature for the bigger and better situated theatres, but with specific criteria defined in this agreement) principals must be full members although chorus may be provisionals. In the non-subsidised repertory agreement, casting is restricted to Equity members (full or provisional) with each member management allowed a quota of four new Equity memberships per year.

Overleaf: Typical form of contract for Equity members engaged under the terms of the various agreements approved by the London Theatre Council and Provincial Theatre Council.

Standard Contract for Provincial Theatre Tours

Approved by Equity and TMA. For implementation from 7th April, 1980, as approved by the Provincial Theatre Council.

PERFORMER'S CONTRACT

Artist's copy WHITE; Equity copy LAVENDER; Manager's copy PINK

THIS CONTRACT IS MADE THIS...day of..19............

BETWEEN...

....(hereinafter called "the Manager") of the one part

AND...(hereinafter called "the Artist")

OF...

....(hereinafter called "the Artist's address") of the other part.

The name and address of the Artist's Agent may be inserted in this space...

The Regulations set out in the Schedules 1 and 2 (except as varied herein) are a part hereof as though set forth herein and shall be binding on the parties hereto.

A COPY OF THE SCHEDULES shall be provided by the Manager to the Equity Deputy and copies thereof are available from the Equity Office.

Engagement *Insert production title if applicable	**1.** The Manager hereby engages the Artist for a Tour of*... ....

*Delete and initial
as necessary

Principals
* (a) To perform the part/s of..
* (b) To perform the part/s of..
  and understudy the part/s of..
* (c) To understudy the part/s of...

* (d) To understudy as required by the Manager.
* (e) To play as cast.
* (f) To play as cast, also "act as known".
* (g) To perform solely the Artist's "act as known".

Chorus
* (i) To perform in the Chorus.
* (j) To perform in the Chorus and understudy as required.
* (k) To perform in the Chorus and understudy the part/s of..
* (l) To understudy as required.
* (m) To understudy the part/s of...
* (n) To perform as: a Flyer/Head Boy or Girl/Swing Dancer.

Period of Engagement

2. (A) The engagement shall commence on the..day of..19..........
or, provided that the Manager gives the Artist not less than eight weeks prior written notice, on some other date not more than seven days before or seven days after that date.

*Two of the Sub-Clauses (i) to (iii) must be deleted and initialled by both parties

(B) The engagement shall be:-
* (i) For the period of rehearsal and the duration of the tour, subject to the Manager giving to the Artist not less than two weeks' written notice of its termination, or paying the Artist two weeks' salary in lieu of such notice.
* (ii) For the period of rehearsal and thereafter until the engagement shall be terminated by either party giving to the other not less than....................days notice in writing (being not less than 14 days) at any time after the Artist's first performance, such notice to expire after the last performance in the working week.
* (iii) For the period of rehearsal and thereafter for a definite period of..consecutive week/s.

*Two of the Sub-Clauses must be deleted and initialled by both parties

(C) The engagement shall be:-
* (i) Once-nightly (8 performances per week).
* (ii) Twice-nightly (12 performances per week).
* (iii) Twice-daily (12 performances per week).

  Note: These expressions are defined in Schedule 1, Clause C6.

Weeks Out
*To be completed or deleted on signing the Contract

(D) (1) The Artist's engagement shall be suspended for the following week/s (hereinafter called "weeks out") commencing*

....

(not being more than one week per complete five weeks of the Artist's engagement).

(2) In respect of any weeks out:-

(a) The Manager shall pay the Artist the relevant minimum weekly performance salary set out in Schedule 1, Appendix 3.

(b) The Manager shall pay the cost of the journey by 2nd class rail from the last venue before the week out to the Artist's address and therefrom to the next venue after the week out.

(c) Paragraph B9, of Schedule 1 hereto shall be suspended so that the Artist shall be entitled to render services for a third party subject to:-

*Complete as applicable

(i) The Artist complying with the following barring Clause in the Manager's Contract with*".."

(ii) The Manager being entitled by giving the Artist prior written notice (not being less than three weeks unless shorter notice is negotiated) either to cancel the week out and continue with the tour of the production or to have first call on the Artist's services during such week for rehearsals when the Artist shall be paid 1/6th of his/her weekly performance salary for each day on which his/her services are so required instead of his/her salary under (D)(2)(a) above for such day/s.

(iii) For the purposes of holiday entitlement a week out shall not be deemed to break the continuity of the Artist's services.

(3) In respect of any Weeks Out for which this Clause 2(D) shall not have been deleted on signing the Contract (hereinafter called "disallowed weeks out") the Manager shall pay the Artist:-

(a) salary in accordance with Clause 3(b) hereof.

(b) at the Manager's option either:-

(i) Touring Allowance in accordance with Schedule 1, Appendix 3 hereof if he/she requires the Artist to remain at the venue OR (if he/she consents to the Artist returning to his/her home).

(ii) the cost of the journey by 2nd class rail from the last venue before the disallowed week out to the Artist's address and thencefrom to the next venue after the disallowed week out.

---

3. The Manager shall pay the Artist:-

Rehearsal Salary

(a) From the commencement of his/her engagement hereunder and thereafter in respect of the first five weeks of rehearsals the sum of £...................per week exclusive of the sums set out in the succeeding sub-clauses of this Clause and in the paragraphs of the Schedule hereto relating to Subsistence and Touring Allowances and Overtime payments.

Performance Salary

(b) From the day of the Artist's first performance and in respect of the sixth and any subsequent weeks of rehearsal the sum of £...................per week, exclusive as in 3(a) above. Note: For minimum salaries see Schedule 1, Appendix 3.

Touring Allowance

(c) A Touring Allowance of £...................per week or part thereof (when on tour) where the Artist's address is 25 miles or more from the rehearsal/performance venue. (For details, see Schedule 1, Appendix 3. See also for details of Daily Touring Allowance).

Understudy Obligation Payments

*(d) If the Artist is engaged to play and understudy under Clause 1 (as distinct from being engaged solely to understudy under Clause 1(c), (d), (l) or (m)) from the day on which his/her understudy duties hereunder are specified £...................per week (being not less than the amount laid down in Schedule 1, Appendix 3) so long as the Artist continues to understudy.

Understudy Performance Payments

*(e) If the Artist performs the part he/she is understudying £...................per performance (being not less than the amounts laid down in Schedule 1, Appendix 3). Provided that the aforesaid payments shall not exceed the limitations of Schedule 1, Appendix 3, Clause E.2.

Head Boy or Girl

*(f) £...................per week for duties as Head Boy or Girl as defined in Schedule 1, from the day on which such duties are specified (being not less than the amount laid down in Schedule 1, Appendix 3).

Swing Dancer

*(g) £...................per week for duties as Swing Dancer, from the day on which such duties are specified (being not less than the amount laid down in Schedule 1, Appendix 3).

Flying
*Complete or delete as applicable

*(h) £...................per week (being not less than the amount laid down in Schedule 1, Appendix 3) if the Artist is required to fly as defined in Schedule 1, from the day he/she is required to fly.

AS WITNESS the hands of the parties on the day, month and year first above written.

....Manager   ....Artist

Manager's Tax Reference No. ....

Artist's N.I. No. ....

Artist's V.A.T. No. (if applicable)..

For and on behalf of ....Ltd.
(Authorised Signatory)

Artist's personal guarantee when Contract made by his/her Limited Company

In consideration of the Manager entering into this Contract I hereby guarantee the compliance by.. Limited of all its obligations under this Contract and I further guarantee personally to comply with all such obligations.

Signed..Artist

Copy of Contract to Equity
A copy of this Contract will be sent to Equity by the Manager unless the Artist notifies the Manager in writing of his/her intention to appeal to Equity against the Manager so doing.

Artist's Equity No. ....Full/Provisional (delete where inapplicable).

Designed by Wm. Pollard & Co. Ltd., Exeter, Devon. B.266

Subsidised repertory or repertoire

There is a separate Equity/TMA agreement applying to managements in receipt of subsidy from ACGB, RAA, local authority etc., presenting plays with a company of whom at least the nucleus are permanent. This agreement has many similar provisions to the other actor contracts despite the tendency for all contracts to phrase differently as a result of different negotiations being conducted by different people at different times.

One provision is a working week constructed from sessions to take account of a pattern that inevitably includes daily rehearsals in addition to performances. Another is the attempt to raise the level of middle salary scales (MRSL): theatres are graded into four categories of average salary that is to be achieved by dividing the total annual salary expenditure by the number of 'actor weeks'.

There is a schedule of variations to take account of the specific problems of children's theatres and 'Theatre in Education' (TIE) companies whose performance patterns and times differ from more traditional theatre.

The casting agreement restricts employment to Equity members (full or provisional) with a quota of two new entry members per year per management.

In accordance with developments in today's theatre, all actor contracts now include an appendix establishing procedures for when the production requires nudity and simulated sex acts.

Alternative theatres

The alternative fringe theatre arose as a reaction against traditional theatre formats and buildings. This, almost by definition, included an initial desire for freedom from the constraints of the sort of small print that is the stuff of contracts. Finance, whether from box-office or from grants, was low and irregular: survival dependent on the sort of deep commitment that can sustain a co-operative. Inevitably, the establishment embraced the more successful fringe elements. Awarded finance became available and with it the whole process of applications which have to be based on budgets. And those budgets have more credibility if their labour costs are based on union approved pay and conditions. Thus the whole contract apparatus is appearing in alternative theatre, at least at its more orthodox end. However there always has been, and for the future development of theatre let us hope that there always will be, a small band of the dedicated who are prepared to starve for a short period in pursuit of ideals that react against current orthodoxy.

There is a 'Contract for Small Scale Producing Venues' agreed between Equity and the ITC incorporating all the basic provisions of the major contracts but with considerably more flexibility, particularly in financial matters. The contract applies to 'approved managers' with the approving body being the Council of Equity — before long there will presumably be a joint union/management body on the lines of the London and Provincial Theatre Councils. Use of this contract is restricted to venues with not more than 250 seats whose managements are not attached to or a part of any subsidised repertory company and have not used, prior to the introduction of this contract, a commercial theatre or subsidised repertory theatre contract.

The casting agreement is that anyone signing this contract, if not already an Equity member, shall immediately apply for membership.

Stage management

All the Equity agreements discussed above include provision for stage management. In general, stage managers are employed on conditions not less favourable than the minimum for actors but with special conditions relating to the nature of stage managment. These recognise that a stage manager has to be on duty before the actors arrive and remain until after the last actors have left; and that some stage management work can only be carried out during actors' breaks. The agreements include minimum staffing numbers and grades with appropriate minimum salary levels. For each agreement there is a standard contract form with clauses appropriate to the stage management sections of the schedules contained in the agreements.

West End casting agreements provide for full Equity membership for Company Stage Managers and Deputy Stage Managers, although ASMs may be provisional. The repertory (subsidised or non-subsidised) agreements specify full or provisional membership with an annual quota of new Technical (i.e. non-acting) ASMs per stage management team, while the Provincial Agreement only specifies Equity membership as a pre-condition for stage management who act or understudy. However the nature of understudying on tour and during seasons makes understudying almost inevitable for the stage management team.

Directors

Equity agreements for directors are fairly recent, dating only from the mid-1970s. One of the stumbling blocks that delayed Equity representation of directors is indicated in the clause on union membership which establishes a procedure for directors who are unwilling to apply for Equity membership on the grounds that they are also managers. In fact this problem appears to be much less than anticipated: many members of TMA are also members of Equity and change hats with a dexterity that is matched by their integrity.

There are two types of directors' contract: one for directors engaged for a season and one for those engaged for a single production. Within this main category, the TMA/Equity agreement further subdivides into subsidised repertory and what might be called 'the rest' — that is, tours or seasons plus commercial rep. These agreements are in the usual Equity format of a contract form agreeing specific terms, supported by a schedule of small print. Thus there are four contract forms to cover the permutations above, plus two simpler contracts for Assistant Directors in respect of subsidised rep and the rest.

Most directors' contracts are based on a preparatory fee, followed by a weekly salary, plus a royalty in the form of a minimum touring fee for weeks when the production plays in a theatre other than the company's home base. The exception is the individual production contract for directing tours and seasons other than rep. Here it is more appropriate to agree a total fee paid by instalments (due at signing, first rehearsal, and first performance) plus a weekly touring royalty for at least week seven onwards. Subsistence, travelling, holiday and illness payments are included in all contracts.

On non-financial matters there are some provisions which reflect the special nature of a director's work. For example, the manager indemnifies the director against civil or criminal prosecution unless the director ignores a written warning from the manager that his treatment of the production is likely to occasion a complaint or claim. A clause in the subsidised rep schedule seeks to clarify the rights of artistic directors — an area of some boardroom friction, perhaps more common in the earlier developing days of the regional theatre movement.

A clause inserted as a precaution rather than one likely to be regularly implemented is: 'Casting for a production shall be a manager's exclusive right and responsibility subject to reasonable consultation with the director where practicable and consideration being given to his view.'

Unless they are 'star directors' with an entitlement to billing in the same size as the title and/or star actor (and therefore presumably with a name which is a box-office asset), directors have the option, without financial penalty, of withdrawing their name from the production if the manager requires substantial changes which the director is not willing to implement, or if the manager makes substantial changes to the production without the director's consent. This is not the road to a successful happy production, but these things do happen and have to be covered in the small print.

The clauses firmly assigning the director's copyright to the manager is an area that is likely to be fought over in the future — and fought with vigour on both sides.

Designers

Designers are the last major section of theatre workers to seek union representation and standard contracts. A Society of Theatre Lighting Designers was formed in 1961, and in 1977 by removal of the word 'lighting' this society was enlarged to include all designers. Discussions were held about possible union representation and an approach was made to Equity who agreed to accept professional employment as a designer to be a qualification for Equity membership. Most of the established designers joined Equity and draft contracts were prepared for presentation to the management associations as the basis of negotiations for a designers' agreement. NATTKE then claimed that they had a prior right to represent designers, especially in the repertory field, and progress was held up while the TUC arbitrated in this inter-union dispute. Eventually it was agreed that both Equity and NATTKE should have a joint right to represent designers and the claims were presented in February 1981. Progress has been slow and some surprise has been expressed at the management associations' apparent tardiness in seeking to reach agreements which would impose formal contractual obligations upon a group of people who can have such a positive effect on the cost effectiveness of theatre production.

Two contracts are proposed: one for designing in repertory and one for individual productions, the first based on salary and the second on fees. These contracts will establish the usual minima in respect of salaries, fees, holidays, illness, expenses, etc.   One new clause relating to particular problems that designers have experienced in the past is headed 'working conditions' and seeks to clarify something that most theatres endeavour to provide as a routine matter of efficient management. For this reason, it is worth reproducing in full:

* All working conditions for designers shall conform to the requirements of the Health and Safety at Work Act and other legislation relating to working conditions.

* Adequate provision shall be made for work and rest places for the Design Department. Work places shall have direct access to adequate natural light and air, and shall be properly heated. All reasonable facilities shall be provided in the work place, including at least one hand basin with hot and cold running water.

* All storerooms shall be adequately ventilated, lit and heated. Scenery, props, costumes, armoury and other equipment shall be stored in a safe manner, and adequate access provided.

* All equipment provided for the Design Department (e.g. paint frames, winches, tallescopes, ladders, etc.) shall be safe and suitably maintained.

* Adequate protective measures shall be taken where the use of certain materials renders such necessary.

Most contentious proposals are the ones whereby the designer retains copyright in the designs, and the one which proposes that 'full details of the total budget for each season/production will be made available to the designer'.

Prior membership of Equity will not be a pre-requisite of engagement as a designer, but application must be made within fourteen days of commencing the engagement.

It is likely that an agreement will have been reached by the time that this book is published.

Technicians

NATTKE has agreements with SWET and TMA. Both agreements recognise that theatres have labour intensive peaks in their operation and that these peaks may occur in irregular patterns depending on the schedule of rehearsals and performaces. This varying labour requirement has inevitably involved a large proportion of casual labour, both backstage and front of house. The trend of negotiations in recent years has been towards consolidating the casual element into regular part-time jobs as far as possible. Thus the agreements deal with (a) full-time staff, (b) performance staff and (c) casual production workers.

As happens in most theatre agreements, the West End is the one most favourable to employees in terms of both wages and conditions and if any regional managers wish to look at their tomorrow, then they should look at the West End's today. This is probably the place to air a personal observation that most of the improvements in working conditions of theatre employees of all kinds have not had disastrous financial or artistic consequences but have improved the total *efficiency* of theatre operations by forcing more attention to be given to scheduling and other matters of forward planning.

There are no specially printed contract forms applicable to either NATTKE/SWET or NATTKE/TMA agreements. The contracts of employment legislation requires that all employees have letter or pro-forma contracts with basic clauses conforming to the requirements of the act. However the NATTKE agreements are based on an understanding that no one will be employed on terms less favourable, and indeed the provisions are the basis of standard working practice throughout the industry.

Full time technical staff work a 40 hour week spread over a rostered 5 out of the 6 weekdays. There is a minimum call of 5 hours in the West End and 4 hours elsewhere with some restrictions on the number of hours within a single day that can be counted towards the basic 40 hour working week. Overtime is paid at time and a half except between midnight and 8 am (11.30 pm until 9 am in the West End) which, with all day Sunday, is at double time rate. In the West End there is a minimum call of 8 hours on Sundays.

The grades of permanent staff to be employed are carefully stipulated in the West End agreement which is also specific on mobility of employees between theatres, particularly those under group management.

Performance staff are paid by the 'show' (up to 3 hours in London, 3½ elsewhere) and there are various clauses to ensure that once a performance pattern for a particular production is established, the performance staff remains constant and is employed on a weekly basis. Subject to working a defined number of weeks per year, regularly employed performance staff are entitled to holiday and sickness pay plus continuation of pay during certain periods of closure. Casual labour is paid on an hourly basis with a minimum call of four hours and, with the exception of production workers in the West End, a maximum of three days in any one week.

The TMA agreement has an alternative repertory schedule which permits an 84 hour working fortnight of any 10 days in 14. This recognises the different pattern of peak production periods in rep. However there are relatively few NATTKE technicians in rep theatres, since much of the technical staffing is carried out by Equity technical ASMs.

Musicians

Both SWET and TMA undertake that only members of the Musicians' Union will be employed in theatre orchestras. Each of the management associations has an agreement (including standard form of contract) with the MU and both agreements have always defined overtime payments very precisely indeed. Theatres have always had to plan optimum use of orchestra time very carefully: however with the tightening up of actor overtime in more recent Equity negotiations, orchestral overtime is no longer quite the overriding consideration that it once was. Indeed rehearsal scheduling has now become an intricate jigsaw of the varying lengths and patterns of calls stipulated by the agreements with different unions.

A theatre musician's weekly salary is based on a specified number of 'performance' sessions: twelve twice nightly or seven once nightly (eight in the West End). These sessions may be performances or rehearsals with appropriate lengths specified accordingly. Additional performances and rehearsals or agreed extensions of sessional time are treated as overtime. Anyone making an orchestra call should study the agreements very carefully to make the most cost-effective use of the varying provisions for matters like intervals, breaks, ready-to-play timings, and seating rehearsals. Other specialist matters covered by MU contracts include:

*   Doubling instruments.
*   Permissible percussion groupings.
*   Playing out of pit, both in and out of audience view.
*   Porterage.

*   Use of recorded music.

*   Broadcasts and recordings.

Writers

Dramatic authors are generally paid in the same way as novelists and other book authors: they receive royalties. In the case of professional performances, this royalty is a percentage of box office receipts, whereas amateur companies generally pay a fixed fee per performance. Once a producing management has decided that a new play is worthy of production, it buys an option giving exclusive rights for a period during which endeavours can be made to find a cast, a production team and an opening date. Plus a theatre if the producer is not theatre-based; and finance if he is a commercial impresario. An option can be extended on further payment or allowed to lapse.

An author's royalties in the West End are likely to be on a sliding scale starting at 5% and rising through 10% as receipts pass agreed break points. A median figure for royalties is probably about 7½%. On the royalties of subsequent rights for tour, rep, amateurs, TV, film etc, the producer of the original production has a sizeable share in acknowledgement of his risk in mounting the first production and his contribution to its success (20% to 30% are common).

Writers are not yet very unionised and contracts are drawn up on an individual basis, negotiated by the author's agents. There are two unions which represent playwrights: The Writers' Guild of Great Britain and The Theatre Writers' Union. These unions have together negotiated the only formal agreements for dramatists: they are agreements with the TNC and apply to productions at the National Theatre, Royal Shakespeare Theatre and the English Stage Company. One agreement deals with normal productions and the other with 'platform plays' covering short plays without decor given by a small cast with minimal costumes and props and separate from the main presentation of the day.

These contracts obviously deal in detail with rights and royalties, but they also establish some of the author's rights in addition to financial provisions, particularly with regard to the following:

*   The writer has the right to attend all rehearsals of the play.

*   No changes in the text submitted may be made except with the writer's permission if the writer is reasonably available for consultation.

*   The producer agrees to rehearse, present and continue to present the play with a cast, director, designer, musical director, choreographer, etc., mutually acceptable to the producer and writer, provided that due consideration shall be given by the writer to the artistic resources of the producer.

* The writer shall be accorded credit similar to that accorded to directors and leading actors in posters, programmes and leaflets.

* The writer reserves the right to use a nom-de-plume provided that it is specified when returning the contract duly signed.

* The writer shall be consulted over programme and all publicity material relating directly to the play that comes under the direct control of the producer, if the writer is reasonably available.

* The writer shall not be required by the producer to perform any function other than that of writer. Specifically the writer shall not be required to act as literary manager, dramaturge, script-reader, or be asked to run workshops.

* The writer shall be given four free seats for the first night of his play and may attend any performance of the play thereafter, free of charge, seating accommodation being subject to the availability thereof.

Performing right

When dramatic and musical works are performed complete, it is relatively straightforward to have a royalty agreement directly between theatre and author/composer. However there are many theatre situations where excerpts ranging from whole musical numbers to mere fragments by several

Collating 'returns' to apportion royalties is a complex process when performances of musical excerpts ranging from whole numbers to mere fragments. The data preparation room at the Performing Right Society's head office (photo: John Rose Associates).

composers are included in the course of a single evening. To simplify the administration of copyright for such performances, writers, composers and publishers have consolidated their rights for such situations in the Performing Right Society. The PRS issue licences and collect royalties for distribution amongst their members.

It is appropriate for theatre buildings to carry an annual licence for overture, entracte and incidental music. Producing managements require licenses for interpolated music and for music used in variety, music hall, pantomimes, concerts, etc. PRS licences are a very complex area: the Performing Right Society publishes extensive explanatory literature but there are many borderline situations which can only be solved by specific enquiry.

Everything that happens on a stage is someone's copyright. In the case of performers this is covered by clauses in their individual service contracts based on union agreements. For writers the copyright is either determined by an individually written contract, or, in virtually every case where there is no such contract, it is subject to collective licensing by the PRS. The trickiest area is when one company performs in a theatre under another company's management. Contracts between producers and theatre managements have clauses determining the responsibility of each for royalty payments. However it is important to remember that, notwithstanding these contractual obligations, the copyright laws impose a joint liability arising from any public performance of copyright music on both theatre producers and 'bricks and mortar' theatre managers.

Use of recordings

The Musicians' Union has an obvious interest in seeking to ensure that, whenever possible, music is played live by musicians present in the theatre rather than from recordings. When commercial sound recordings are used for interval and dentracte music a licence is required from Phonographic Performance Ltd: there are appropriate tariffs for different purposes such as incidental music in professional plays, concert interval music, amateur productions, etc. Where commercial recordings are re-recorded on to tape, even when done purely for technical convenience, an additional licence may be required from the Mechanical Protection Society Ltd.

8   Contracting theatres

The manufactured production has to be retailed to its audience. The building based companies — about eighty in Great Britain — do this in their own theatre. But the majority have to perform in theatres where the producing company has the status of temporary tenant under a wide range of possible agreements with the landlord.

In the West End

In the West End, the producing company pays a rent to the theatre. This rent is based on a percentage of box office receipts with a guaranteed minimum. The production company also takes over most of the running costs of the theatre including staff, lighting and heating. Thus the theatre landlord stands to share in any success through the percentage element in the rental and through the increased bar and catering sales resulting from a fuller house. However the landlord does not risk sharing in any failure: the theatre is largely immunised from loss by the guarantee element in the rental and by the producer assuming the theatre's running costs during the tenancy. Moreover the contracts include a clause allowing the theatre to give notice to terminate if the takings fall below a specified level.

In times of West End prosperity, with shows queueing for theatres, the dice were nicely loaded in favour of the landlord. In current harder times, the rental terms have to be more finely tuned, especially in the less favourably situated houses and so a succession of flop rentals can spell losses for the landlord.

In the interests of culture and tourism, it is difficult to see how the West End can survive without an injection of awarded cash. This has already started in a small way since many West End productions are now transfers from subsidised theatres where the initial production cost risks have been cushioned by awarded funds.

In the regions

The range of performances toured to mixed programme theatres and arts centres is now so wide that the word 'product' is becoming established as the general term to cover performances of all possible types. Theatre's neat traditional classifications such as drama, opera, ballet, variety, musical etc.

are no longer sufficient: many productions now span the whole range of traditional performance skills, plus a few skills so new that they await definition. The boundaries are indistinct: even a previously straightforward descriptive word like 'concert' has become so wide in its application as to be virtually meaningless. Types of performances are now as wide as the range of places where these performances are staged: it is hardly surprising that the 1981 Harrogate Arts and Entertainment Conference had a major session entitled 'Product Meets Venue'. No matter how much reluctance we may feel at having Shakespeare classified as a consumer product, there is a considerable logic in this since there are so many marketing techniques common to both bard and baked beans. So how does product meet venue and how do the two parties negotiate a contract for that meeting?

Wholesalers and agents

There are very few wholesalers in the theatre industry and they operate mainly in the music business where acts are sometimes bought and combined into packages for sale to venues. The normal intermediaries between product and venue are agents who are paid commission by the producing organisation for securing bookings and negotiating the financial and other contract terms.

This practice is now confined mainly to solo performers and small groups. When the conventional weekly touring circuits were the main force in regional theatre, there were agents who specialised in arranging standard tours of plays and musicals throughout the theatre towns in a logical (i.e. economic) sequence.

Arts Council

Some of this role has been taken over by the Arts Council Touring Department who are responsible for ensuring that the visits of the subsidised opera, dance and drama companies are equitably distributed throughout the regions in terms of seasons and repertoire as well as geography. The visits of the major companies are virtually 'allocated' by the Arts Council. The ACGB Touring Department are also able to assist some commercial tours of approved plays by making available funds to lower the required guarantee to a more viable figure for approved venues.

Regional Arts Associations

When RAAs support regionally based companies by accepting responsibility for a major portion of the funding, they help to coordinate bookings to try to ensure that such companies make the optimum contribution to the region's theatrical life. They also play a similar coordinating role for the companies that they encourage to visit the region by offering financial assistance to close the gap between the fee that the regional venues can afford, and the fees that such companies would be compelled to charge if they relied only upon their central Arts Council funding.

The RAAs are now cooperating in the development of a series of grid venue schemes, particularly for small-scale touring, with the aim of reducing travel and publicity costs by bringing companies to the region for a concentrated series of geographically convenient performances. Such tours are often arranged to radiate from a residency in an appropriate centre and to include such supporting activities as workshop sessions.

Direct contact

By far the greatest proportion of contacts between product and potential venue are by direct negotiation. There may be preliminary correspondence but the final details are inevitably settled by telephone negotiation prior to a confirmatory exchange of contracts.

Negotiating terms

Both for a company trying to arrange a tour and for a theatre trying to put together a season, the process of negotiation is something of an obstacle race. The company is anxious to arrange dates in a logical geographical sequence while the theatre requires a balanced programme with classics and contemporaries evenly spread, mainstream in just proportion to alternative, music and dance at regular intervals, Shakespeare that matches the exam syllabus, plus the mandatory annual fixes of Ayckbourn and Agatha.

While both sides juggle with their schedules there is an escalation of commitment which may be summarised in the following jargon phrases which are often used to indicate progress, both in conversation and on planning charts:

Interested
Light Pencil
Pencil
Heavy Pencil
Agreed
▼ Contracted

The company hopes for a better financial deal than the theatre is ever prepared to offer: both want the other to bear the risk. How then do we bridge the gap between what the theatre wants to give and what the company wants to take? There are several possible contractual arrangements that can form the basis for the inevitable haggling.

Fees and rentals

The production company may charge a fixed fee. In this case the theatre takes the risk, sharing with the company neither the loss nor profit that may result from variations in the size of the audience. Similarly, the theatre may charge a fixed rent, leaving the production company to take the risk of a loss of the box office falls below the rental figure — a potential loss that the production company must weigh against the possibility of pocketing any box office receipts in excess of the rent if the attendances are good. Fees and rentals are only attractive to the production that can command a big fee or to the theatre that can charge a big rent.

Percentages

Most deals, however, involve some degree of risk sharing. The traditional method of percentages shared the risk by splitting the box office takings between production company and theatre in an agreed proportion. This method is still used, often with a split of 65% to the production company and 35% to the theatre, although this may be dropped to 60/40 or raised to 70/30 or even 75/25. The agents of major stars (the kind who sit on a stool and get chummy with the audience) might try asking for something approaching 95/5 and even stand some hope of getting it.

Guaranteed percentages

Straight percentage deals were a mutually agreeable solution in the heyday of the touring circuits when normal attendances produced enough revenue to meet, with some certainty, the costs of both production and theatre. Indeed a good Saturday plus a reasonable Friday could cover the outgoings, leaving the rest of the week as profit. But with rising costs and falling attendances, the touring circuits began to decline. Straight percentage agreements depend on a mutual confidence that the company side will strive for a high standard of production while the theatre side will maintain the comfort of the building and pursue an active marketing policy to fill the seats. Soon there was a downward spiral with losses in standards, attendances and confidence all interacting to mutual disadvantage. The main force in arresting the decline was the introduction of the guarantee as a standard practice. The agreement then became one where the visiting company receives an agreed percentage of the box office receipts, but the theatre guarantees that this shall not be less than an agreed sum. The negotiating jargon for discussing this kind of deal is 'guarantee £4,000 against 65%' or even just '4 against

65'. The understanding among producing and theatre management members of the Theatre Management Association is that guarantees should not exceed the sum to break even — that is, the actual weekly running cost plus a sum to amortise the production costs, calculated by dividing the number of touring weeks into the total production costs. A theatre manager is entitled to have sight of the touring manager's budget breakdown but rarely exercises this right.

First calls

By ensuring that the producer can depend on his share not falling below a known amount, the guarantee system encourages maintenance of production standards. However it does leave the theatre rather exposed to the risk of the production turning out to be a poor audience puller. As most tours have to be negotiated prior to rehearsal, guarantees must inevitably be negotiated in a spirit of faith, hope and intuition. And totalled guarantees for a season can be quite a formidable burden on an enterprise which has to rely on deficit funding. A useful alternative to the guarantee is the 'first call' with the visitors being entitled to the first £X,000 of box office receipts while the theatre has the next £Y,000 with a percentage split thereafter. This limits the theatre's potential loss to the possibility of receiving a nil box office share.

   If the theatre is guaranteeing and thus bearing the risk, it will try for a high percentage. If the show is likely to be a hit, it is in the theatre's interest to offer a guarantee and thus seek to retain a high percentage — but vice versa for the production company. If the show is a doubtful puller, the whole situation reverses. It is pure cat and mouse where bluff and counter-bluff are the weapons with repartee inevitably resorting to such lines as 'Well, if you have so much faith in the audience pull of your show, why do you need such a big guarantee?'

Guarantees to the theatre

As we have already noted, in the West End the guarantees are in favour of the theatres which are let on a basis of a percentage of box office income with a guaranteed minimum. However, on tour the guarantee is invariably by the theatre to the production. The one possible exception is amateur productions in professional theatres where the theatre may seek minimum guaranteed receipts on account of its box office percentage, or charge a basic rental plus a further sliding rental in the form of a percentage.

Contras

The rent for a West End theatre does not cover much more than the use of the building and its equipment. The producer has to assume responsibility for the salaries of the theatre staff. On tour, the theatre meets most of the staff costs and this is reflected in the higher percentages sought by the touring theatres. Touring stage staff costs, particularly overtime, are subject to negotiations: traditionally the theatres meet the cost of a Monday get-in plus the cost of performance staff, with any Sunday work being a shared cost. However everything has now become flexible with old concepts of both product and venue widening to embrace almost anything playing anywhere.

One responsibility that, with the very few exceptions of an occasional municipal theatre, still remains firmly in the touring manager's wallet is the get-out. With the fall of the curtain on the final performance, the technical staff cease working for the theatre. Dismantling and loading is paid for by the touring manager as a lump sum per man. This is negotiated with the touring manager along guidelines suggested by union agreement but usually increased to reflect the fact that loading trucks at 2 am on a Sunday morning, probably in the cold and possibly in the rain, is hardly an attractive occupation for a skilled technical crew who have already worked two Saturday performances.

Advertising is another item for sharing. In traditional weekly touring, the company produced posters and leaflets as requisitioned by the theatre who were then responsible for distribution and display. Newspaper advertising was shared. With so many changes in the system, not just in products and venues but with the increasing proportion of runs of less than a week, the whole thing has become something of a mess of individual practices. The simplest way is to agree 'no contras' subject to the touring company supplying a mutually agreed amount of print and undertaking to keep technical staff calls to a minimum, while the theatre promises to use its best endeavours to market the show.

Contracts

After terms have been agreed by negotiation, contracts have to be exchanged between theatre and company. These are normally issued by the theatre. However contracts can be issued by the agents of some acts, particularly musical packages making concert tours which include venues where performances are irregular and there is a consequent lack of experienced management staff to ensure that the formal paperwork is carried out.

Prior to 1981, contracts were not standardised although the small print in each individual contract covered common essential requirements such as responsibilites for insurance, licenses, royalties, etc. The TMA has now produced a standard contract, approved for use by its members whether in charge of theatres (resident managers) or production companies (visiting managers). This contract was drawn up by a working party who not only standardised the items in existing contracts but took into account changing needs in the light of the widening definitions of both product and venue.

Standard contracts are efficient management tools since they save a great deal of time that otherwise has to be spent in studying the details of printed clauses if every organisation has their own individual wording. This TMA contract is very comprehensive and a careful study of it will reveal a great deal about the relationships between a theatre and the production that it is buying — including the points to be negotiated and the matters requiring organisation by both parties.

STANDARD CONTRACT AS APPROVED BY THE TMA

THE LITTLE THEATRE
Small Street, Lilliput, LT1 1TL.
Tel: (0999) 9876
General Manager: Lemuel Gulliver

(Vat Registration No: 123 4567 89)

_____

1. THIS CONTRACT is made
    the _____ day of _____ 19____
    BETWEEN   The   Little   Theatre,   Lilliput   (The   Resident   Manager)   and
    _____ (The Visiting Manager)
    WHEREBY The Visiting Manager agrees to produce
    _____ IN _____
    the engagement to commence on
    _____ and the production to open on _____
    and terminate on
    _____   (SCHEDULE 1)

    The Visiting Manager further agrees not to allow the production to be performed in any medium within _____ miles of Lilliput within _____ weeks prior to, during or for _____ weeks after the termination of the engagement.
    This Contract is subject to the terms and conditions following and the Schedules attached.

2. TERMS
    a) The production shall include the following named artists:
    _____
    _____

    (The failure of a named artist to appear shall constitute grounds for the termination of this contract and/or the imposing of such penalties as may be detailed in SCHEDULE 2)

b) The Visiting Manager shall

   i) Pay the Resident Manager a fee/rental of _____ (*delete as appropriate)

  ii) Receive a fee of _____

 iii) Receive a guaranteed payment of _____ against _____ % of the Box Office receipts net of VAT and Discount.

 iv) Receive _____ % of the Box Office receipts net of VAT and Discount.

  v) _____

_____

(Four of these sub-clauses to be struck out)
such sum, less any advances and payments due under the contra account (SCHEDULE 2), to be paid not later than _____ days after the mutual agreement of the Contra Account. In the event of failure to agree on the Contra Account within _____ days from the end of the engagement the Resident Manager shall forthwith pay to the Visiting Manager the sum not in dispute.

3.   VISITING MANAGER'S RESPONSIBILITIES
The Visiting Manager shall
a) Provide the production at his own expense.
b) Provide a full and efficient company capable of presenting the production and with reasonable provision for understudies.
c) Provide all properties, costumes, scenery, furniture, band parts and instruments, and shall provide storage for the same at his own expense if no space is available in the Theatre. (SCHEDULE 3)
d) Obtain in respect of the production (and indemnify the Resident Manager against) all necessary licences or permissions, and pay all copyright royalties, or other fees in respect thereof other than fees payable by the Resident Manager under PRS Tariff T for overture, entr'acte and incidental music.
e) Provide on demand in advance a copy of the actual script to be performed together with scene and lighting plots and requisitions for technical staff by the date specified. (SCHEDULE 3)
f) Provide on demand, where a guaranteed payment is agreed, a detailed breakdown of the sum guaranteed under Clause 2(b) (iii).

4.   RESIDENT MANAGER'S RESPONSIBILITIES
The Resident Manager shall
a) Provide the theatre, together with all technical equipment and stock scenery as normally installed, with all heating and lighting as normally available. (SCHEDULE 4).
b) Provide and pay for administrative, front of house and cleaning staff as required for the proper and efficient running of the Theatre (save unavoidable absence which may be caused by yillness, strike, lock-out, dispute or force majeure).
c) Provide and pay for technical staff within the limits specified. (SCHEDULE 4).
d) Obtain in respect of the theatre all necessary licences or permissions.
e) Receive and bank the Box Office receipts, and provide the Visiting Manager on demand with true accounts thereof on a daily basis with weekly summaries.

5.   MUTUAL RESPONSIBILITIES

The Resident Manager and the Visiting Manager shall

a) Respectively effect and maintain adequate insurance policies to cover all requisite Statutory and other Legal Liability as follows:

  (i) The Resident Manager shall be responsible for such cover against all risks in respect of his property, and that for which he is responsible, his employees, and members of the public provided that the Resident Manager shall not be responsible for loss or theft of or damage to the property belonging to the Visiting Manager or employees of the Visiting Manager.

  (ii) In any case not attributable to negligence on the part of the Resident Manager the Visiting Manager shall be responsible for such cover in respect of his employees and members of the public and against all risks in respect of his property and that of his employees arising out of his use and occupancy of the Theatre.

b) Not do or suffer to be done in or about the premises anything whereby any policy of insurance effected by the other may be invalidated or which may cause any increased premium to become payable for such insurance, but shall at all times use all proper precautions to prevent loss, or damage or harm by fire or accident.

c) Each ensure that they and all their employees and agents observe, carry out and abide by all conditions and regulations imposed by Statute or any competent Authority with reference to or in connection with the Theatre or any performance therein and in particular to observe all fire and safety regulations including the fire proofing of the production to meet local requirements. (SCHEDULE 5).

6.   MARKETING AND PUBLICITY

a) Seat Prices:	Prices of admission and concessions to parties children and offers below these prices of admission shall be fixed by the Resident Manager only after consultation with the Visiting Manager whose advice shall not unreasonably be ignored.
b) Print:	Unless otherwise agreed and noted in SCHEDULE 6 of this Contract the Visiting Manager shall provide by the date specified, posters, hanging cards and leaflets to agreed sizes and in the agreed quantities, all properly headed and dated, and at the same time provide photographs, biographies and publicity material, all in accordance with SCHEDULE 6, of which effective use shall be made.
c) Media Advertising:	The Visiting Manager agrees to pay towards such cost of preliminary and current newspaper advertising, locally handwritten bills, local radio and TV advertising and such other local publicity commitments all as may be specified in the sum or proportion specified in SCHEDULE 6.
d) Press Calls:	The Visiting Manager agrees to use his best efforts to secure the participation of his contracted artistes in such press, radio or TV interviews, photo calls or publicity appearances as the Resident Manager may reasonably arrange.

e) Programmes: Unless otherwise agreed and noted in SCHEDULE 6 of this Contract the Resident Manager shall be responsible for the printing and sale of programmes. The programme material shall be agreed between the Resident Manager and the Visiting Manager. The Visiting Manager shall deliver programme material to the Resident Manager by the date specified in SCHEDULE 6.

7. CONTROL AND PROTECTION

a) The Resident Manager reserves the right to:
  i) superintend and control the Theatre for the protection, accommodation and convenience of the public, and for the fulfilment of all obligations, terms and conditions of any and all licences relating to the Theatre;
  ii) object, in order to protect himself under the Theatres Act, to any song, speech, dialogue, business, costume or gesture and the same shall be withdrawn or altered as the Resident Manager may direct.
b) The Visiting Manager agrees that neither he nor any member of his Company shall personally address the audience, interfere in any manner with other artistes or employees, or go into the front of house, without permission of the Resident Manager.
c) The Resident Manager shall be exclusively entitled to the income from the exercise of all front of house privileges, including revenue from the sale of programmes, its own souvenir articles, and revenue from Bars and refreshment rooms (SCHEDULE 7).
d) The Visiting Manager agrees to observe, carry out and abide by all general rules particular to the Theatre and any other rules for the time being in force at the Theatre. (SCHEDULE 7).

8. GENERAL PROVISIONS

a) Cancellation
  (i) If there shall be some supervening event which shall render this Contract incapable of being performed in the manner reasonably contemplated by the parties then this Contract shall be suspended for as long as such incapacity shall continue or for the duration of the engagement hereunder (whichever period shall be shorter) and any payments due shall be apportioned by mutual agreement.
  (ii) In the event of failure by the Visiting Manager to fulfil the obligations on his part herein contained, the Resident Manager will use his best endeavours to minimise his loss, but subject thereto the Visiting Manager will remain liable to the Management for all payments, costs and outlays hereby contracted for, in which event payments due to or by the Visiting Manager in terms hereof will be reasonably adjusted in respect of the particular circumstances.
b) The Schedules
  The Schedules attached to this Contract shall be read as though they were part of the Contract.
c) Serving of Notices
  It is mutually agreed as follows
  Any notice which the Resident Manager may desire or be required to give to the Visiting Manager hereunder shall be deemed to be duly given if sent by registered post to the Visiting Manager or left for the Visiting Manager at the Theatre during this engagement and any notice which the Visiting Manager may desire or be required to give to the Resident

Manager hereunder shall be deemed to have reached the party for whom it was intended at the time when in the ordinary course of post it should have been delivered, and in proving service by post it shall be sufficient to prove that the notice was addressed in the prescribed manner and was registered.

d) This Contract being personal to the parties hereto shall not, nor shall the benefits thereof, be assigned to underlet by either party, nor shall any person or Company be substituted to carry out the obligations hereby undertaken by either party without the consent in writing of the other.

e) Nothing herein contained shall be deemed to constitute a partnership between the parties.

9. ARBITRATION

Any dispute arising out of this Contract shall be referred for a binding decision to the Theatrical Management Association ("the TMA"), if the parties agree, and in default of agreement to a single Arbitrator to be appointed (in default of agreement) by the President for the time being of the TMA subject to the provisions of the Arbitration Acts of 1950 and 1979.

CONCLUSION

This document reflecting the terms and conditions verbally agreed between the parties shall be submitted in duplicate to the Visiting Manager signed on behalf of the Resident Manager and one copy thereof shall be returned to the Resident Manager within the ensuing 14 days signed on behalf of the Visiting Manager so as to constitute a contract between the parties.

Signed by the said Lemuel Gulliver
as the representative of the Little   in the presence of:
Theatre, Lilliput:

_____   _____

Signed by the said_____
being the Visiting Manager or
Representative thereof: in the presence of:

_____   _____

Address: ....
....
    Telephone:...
    VAT Registration No:..
    I am/am not a member of the Theatrical Management Association

Schedules

The Schedules are intended to be set out by individual managements to meet their particular needs.

They should, however, be in the following order and make provision for at least the following headings, so as to meet the requirements of the main body of the Contract. Brackets round a sub-heading (usually penalty clauses) indicate areas which are not common to the majority of existing contracts but which have been strongly recommended to the Working Party for inclusion.

SCHEDULE 1	Get-in day and time
	Rehearsals
	Performance days and times
	Get-out day and time
	(Provision for settlement within reasonable time subject to penalty clause)
SCHEDULE 2	Advance payments
	Payment for get-in
	Payment for resident staff overtime
	Payment for performance staff
	Payment for publicity
	Payment for get-out
	Payment for piano tuning, telephone calls, stage supplies etc.
	Named artists
	(a) Penalties
	(b) Illness
	(c) Refunds
SCHEDULE 3	Technical requirements including seat removals and time and penalty clauses. Storage of set.
SCHEDULE 4	Hours and availability and numbers of resident staff for which Resident Manager pays. Normal stage (electrical and sound) equipment, heating and lighting equipment. Piano.
SCHEDULE 5	Details of local authority licensing in respect of fire-proofing, naked lights etc.
SCHEDULE 6	Programme copy: (Time and penalty clause)
	Special wording
	Admission prices
	Concessions
	Complimentaries
	Number of posters, hanging cards, leaflets and photographs required.
	(Re: publicity material listed in Clause 6(b) a time clause and percentage penalty payment)
	Share of press advertising, provision for schedule of advertising and proof of payment thereof included in publicity contra.
SCHEDULE 7	Special local rules, i.e. rules appropriate to particular managements/companies.
	Latecomers. Merchandise.

9   Information and image

Once a product has been designed, manufactured and distributed to its retail outlets, it has to be sold to buyers. The process of making potential buyers aware of their need for this unique and indispensable product has come to be known as 'marketing'. Where marketing ends and selling begins is unclear and varies not just between one industry and another but between different organisations within the same industry. Many organisations pride themselves upon being market-oriented, meaning that they only make what the customer has been discovered by market research to want; and to a design that incorporates the lowest common denominator requirements of the 'market sector' that is 'target' for the product.

This approach is inappropriate for a product which is connected in any way, however tenuous, with the process of education. Nevertheless, however lofty an arts organisation's aims may be, there is always some necessity to take market requirements into account — and to research that market by some process however informal or primitive — because no performance is complete until it has communicated with an audience. Moreover, sheer survival requires an average audience in excess of at least some 70% upwards to avoid disenchantment on the part of the vital subsidising bodies.

There is a cynical definition of marketing which runs 'selling people something that they do not need'. A more accurate and palatable definition is 'selling people something that they did not realise that they needed'. The word 'marketing' first came into theatre as a description for something that has always been done in one form or another with varying degrees of commitment. The appearance of marketing staff, either as additional appointments or the redesignation of existing personnel, lead to a more systematic approach involving a study of techniques used in other consumer industries, and their experimental use towards incorporation in theatre practice.

Audience getting

Assuming that the theatre has a programme of acceptable standard, getting an audience for it involves a four part process:

* Getting the potential audience to know what the show is and what it is about.

* Getting them to want to see it.

*   Encouraging them to buy a ticket.

*   Selling them that ticket.

Parts 3 & 4 of this process are discussed in the next chapter since they are associated with the box office operation. Parts 1 & 2 are mainly a matter of what is usually labelled as 'press and publicity' or variations thereof. However a more useful working phrase is 'information and image' because it conveys the purpose of any publicity and public relations operation. The word 'image' must never be used publicly because it puts both press and audience on their guard against the very sort of image that one is trying to create. But an overall image is vital.

A theatre's image has to be (a) identifiable and (b) convey success. Audience loyalty depends on their ability to identify with a theatre whose policies and attitudes are clearly defined and presented. And success can widen the range of public acceptance and approval — even from those who may view the expressed policies and attitudes with less than enthusiasm.

Information is conveyed to the potential audience by means of advertising and editorial coverage in the media; and by various kinds of printed matter produced for display or distribution. The information is presented in such a way as to help convey the theatre's desired image.

Advertising and editorial

Information and image are closely interlinked, but for securing them there is another subdivision that is not interlinked: the advertising space that is paid for and the editorial space that is free. In theory at least, advertising and editorial are not linked. But in practice, particularly in local papers, there is a recognition that editorial on specialised subjects attracts specialised readers who in turn attract specialised advertisers. And conversely, if a subject is considered worth advertising, then there must surely be enough interested readers around to warrant allocation of some editorial space. But these rationalisations are never referred to in discussion or correspondence. Advertising and editorial must be kept apart:

*   Never talk to editorial staff about adverts.

*   Or talk to ad reps about editorial.

*   Never enclose advertising copy and editorial matter in the same envelope.

Advertising

Newspapers

There are two types of newspaper advertising: classified and display. Every theatre needs to appear in the entertainments section of the classified of its local paper. This is where the regular audience will look to check what's on. It is also the part of the paper that will be looked over by the casual audience considering a possible night out.

These adverts should be placed in a fixed position and have a fixed format. They can be single or double column width. A regional playhouse with three-weekly runs may find that double column gives a better layout when the copy only includes the current play, the next one, and possibly a couple of Sunday concerts. However a mixed programme theatre with a high proportion of one, two and three nighters may find that a single column gives a clearer layout in the column centimetres possible within the budget. Such an advert will be headed by a regular distinctive block, possibly including a logo, but certainly using a distinctive typeface, perhaps reversed to read white against a black background. Either at top or bottom should be the box-office telephone number and possibly box-office opening hours. Then for each production there should be dates, time and price range. It is useful to include a pithy phrase summarising the type of show: not so much as a 'come on' but more to help potential audience decide whether or not the show is the type of entertainment that they are seeking on a particular occasion. A recognisable star is useful, remembering that actors are not the only kind of star names: authors like Agatha Christie and ensembles like the Royal Shakespeare Company can be bigger pullers than mere actors. Several alternative theatre companies have built national reputations and many others have a local following through working extensively within a region. This makes them stars. The requirement for a classified theatre ad is to find the minimum number of words that will inform on the nature of the production while selling it as an attractive proposition.

Display adverts are a back-up to the regular informative classified advertising. They may appear in the entertainment pages to give a more detailed selling message on a particular production, but they are more often included to catch the eye of the more casual reader who is not specifically looking for a night out. They may be placed on weekly arts and entertainment editorial pages or, more often, just in random 'run of the paper' positions. It is often possible to get particularly favourable positions in newspapers on the fringe of your local area. There is a mutual interest: they wish to extend their advertising area, and you wish to extend your audience catchment area.

Display ads in monthlies, especially in the glossier 'dentist's waiting room' types of publication with a long life, are more effective when they convey a more general message about theatre policy with outline of the season and details of how to get more precise information. Theatres tend to splash out on advertising space when announcing a new season: they may go for a dramatic long single column, or perhaps a half or full page ad, possibly using a second colour or even full colour. If the season includes

Theatre ROYAL

Tel. Norwich 28205/6/7

BOX OFFICE OPEN DAILY
10 a m 9 p m MON SAT

GOOD SEATS AVAILABLE

LAST 3 DAYS
Ends Aug. 28th. Nightly 8.15
Sat. 6 and 8.40
"REJOICE, REJOICE
GODSPELL
IS
MAGNIFICENT"
THE ALL-FAMILY MUSICAL
Prices: £2-£4.50

Comm. Sept. 27th. Nightly
7.30. Mat. Wed. & Sat. 2.30
NATIONAL THEATRE present
**THE IMPORTANCE OF
BEING EARNEST**
Starring Judi Dench, Nigel
Havers, Anna Massey, Paul
Rogers, Zoe Wannamaker
£2.50-£5.50. Mon. eve. & Sat.
mat. £2-£4. Wed. mat. £2.50

Comm. Oct. 18th. Nightly 8
p.m. Sat. 5 and 8 p.m.
WAYNE SLEEP with **DASH**
A dynamic dance programme

Sunday, Nov. 28th, 7.30
THE CHIEFTAINS

Britain's Greatest Panto
MOTHER GOOSE
Kathy Staff (TVs Nora Batty and
Doris Luke), **Bobby Bennett** (TVs
Junior Showtime)
NOW BOOKING

Delicious freshly-made **Coffee**
and **Danish Pastries**, **Salads**,
Ploughman Lunch and **Daily**
Hot Special Toasted
Sandwiches, Filled Rolls. The
best cup of coffee in town.
All day service 10 a.m.-9 p.m.

CIRCLE BAR open for sale of
liquor and soft drinks
11.30 a.m.-2.30; 5.30-11 p.m.

**VISIT OUR COFFEE SHOP
AND FOOD BAR**

Daily newspaper classified advert for a regional mixed programme touring theatre.

Display advert in the same newspaper to back up the selling message for particular production.

**THE LONGEST RUNNING
CHRISTMAS COMEDY
OF ALL TIME . . .**

NOW IN ITS
381st YEAR!

Now booking to 15 Jan '83
All seats £4.90 (pre Christmas)

with Suzan Farmer   Edward Petherbridge
John Fraser   Sarah Porter
Simon Gipps-Kent   Gary Raymond
Edward Hardwicke   Emily Richard

William Shakespeare's
TWELFTH NIGHT
DONMAR WAREHOUSE THEATRE
41 Earlham Street, London WC2 tel. 01-379 6565/836 1071
Covent Garden

A good display ad combining an eye-catching joke with factual information on what, who, when, where . . . plus a 'how much' that encourages early booking to save money.

BOOKING NOW OPEN

THEATRE ROYAL, NORWICH
Box Office (0603) 28205/6/7
From 27 Sept for 8 perfs only

**NATIONAL
THEATRE
company in**

Oscar Wilde's
masterpiece

The Importance of Being Earnest

Cast : Judi Dench, Elizabeth Garvie,
John Gill, Nigel Havers, Martin Jarvis,
Brian Kent, Anna Massey, Paul Rogers,
Zoë Wanamaker
Director Peter Hall
Design and Lighting by John Bury

NT DIRECT FROM THE
NATIONAL THEATRE LONDON

Perfs Mon to Sat 7.30, Wed & Sat mat 2.30
Prices from £2.50 to £5.50
ARTS COUNCIL TOUR

substantial discounts, then such ads will feature distinctive 'Subscribe Now!!' messages.

All advertising is subject, as is billing of all kinds, to the individual contracts of actors, authors, directors, designers and even impresarios. However this is more likely to affect the advertising of West End productions than others. Billing clauses often work on a cascade system: X's billing is guaranteed when Y's name appears, and Y's billing is subject to Z being included and so on. Clever producers devise crafty chains that can be broken after the meaningful names in display ads. However if the star, or the author or director, are big enough to be able to insist on inclusion in adverts, then their name is usually worth having there.

Television

The advertising medium with the widest and most positive impact is television. The specially made commercials of production highlights that help to build Broadway long runs have not yet become standard elsewhere. However regional theatres have built successful campaigns on ten second exposures of a static slide with a crisp-selling voiceover. Apart from selling a particular show, mere appearance amongst the big advertisers during television commercial breaks implies success and therefore contributes to a theatre's overall image. This technique has been used to particular effect by Norwich Theatre Royal with slide images in that theatre's characteristic fairground style of graphics and colouring which give continuity to all its publicity.

Television advertising cannot replace the information service of newspaper classifieds: it is to be considered as part of a display campaign. At first sight the equation of a few seconds of TV time versus many column centimetres of newsprint may look unpromising. And certainly TV is potentially more effective and justifiable for a larger theatre where a smaller percentage increase in seat occupancy represents a substantial number of seats. However ten seconds is a long time in television terms and it seems that this form of advertising will gradually play an increasingly positive role.

Another form of TV advertising that we may see develop is the regional campaign, possibly with the Regional Arts Associations playing both a coordinating and financially supportive role, to sell the general appeal of all the region's theatres while spotting certain individual productions.

Radio

In areas where independent local radio is available, advertising is available at rates which do not look horrific when compared with local newspapers. And they appear quite positive in their cost effectiveness when one contemplates all the motorists and housewifes who constitute a captive audience, especially when one considers that they are probably using radio as a background to boring routine tasks. Just the moment to sell the idea of a night out.

Editorial

Newspapers and magazines consist of acres of blank white paper needing to be filled with news. Radio and television are silent air space waiting to be filled. Theatres need to inform readers and listeners. With the media looking for news and the theatres generating news we surely have the basis of a useful mutual dependency!

Reviews

Editorial coverage of theatre divides into news and reviews. Of course a review is news — if published the morning after the first night, it is probably the most genuine news to emanate from a theatre in that it will inform about the production faster than the word of mouth from the first night audience. But the difference between a review and other news is the extent of control that the theatre has over it. We can try by various devices to manipulate the treatment of news by attempting to influence reporters by the way in which we present the theatre's case. But dealings with reviewers need to be conducted with respect for the ethics that surround the business of criticism, and indeed give it its credibility.

Theatres need critics to review shows. A bad review may not help a theatre to fill seats but at least it keeps the theatre's name before the public. And surely every theatre must proceed on the assumption that its next production is always going to be excellent. So there is never a need to discuss whether to invite reviewers: the question is how to make sure that they will come. This requires a two-pronged attack. The first is merely part of the general need to make sure that your theatre and its activities are considered to be an area of reader interest. The second is to smooth the critic's progress by attention to such details as:

* Invite in writing and follow up by telephone as appropriate. Local paper critics will receive regular news releases of their local theatre's first nights and will either ring in for seats or have to be rung to check whether they are coming.

* Establish whether seats are to be sent or collected on arrival.

* Give good seats in the reviewer's preferred section of the house. Seat should be on the gangway — may need a fast getaway to meet a deadline. And in a small town, the critic may be the duty reporter liable to be called to a fire big enough to upstage your first night.

* Never seat critics together unless they have specially requested this.

* You cannot influence critics, but it can be useful if advance press information includes some kindly critical quotes from earlier touring dates, or previous productions of the play.

* A critic needs an 'angle' to his notice. It is legitimate to 'feed' a local paper critic who is not a theatre enthusiast and whose notice is just one of a whole series of bits of copy to be written against tonight's deadline. Local angles, personality angles etc. can be dropped into telephone conversations. Or there may be a 'how the show nearly didn't go on'. (The curtain was embarrassingly delayed, and the audience a touch restive, on the start of an eminent actor's one man show — a whispered 'he can't get his beard to stick' ensured that the notice was treated by the sub-editors as news worthy of a banner headline in a prominent position on the leader page.

* Welcome the reviewer in the foyer. You are genuinely pleased to see him and so this will show. Have a copy of the programme ready and find out which drink he would like in the interval. Do not talk about the show.

* Make sure he gets the pre-ordered interval drink. Leave him alone if he wants to think, although a local paper's critic may also be the theatre reporter and interested in talking about the next show or sounding out on any theatre problem like deficits and the state of relations with Councillor Bloggs. But never talk about the current show except to answer questions.

* Make sure that the box office take calls and relay them immediately through the house manager.

* Make telephone lines available for phoning in copy if required.

* Do not be upset if a critic has to leave before the end — just be relieved that he cannot then morally write a really bad notice.

* If, after the critic has left prematurely, an actor breaks a leg, the set falls over or the theatre burns down, telephone the critic and tell him.

Press release

The standard way of passing news announcements to the media is by circulating a document called a 'press release'. The news may be for immediate release or its use may be subject to an embargo until a stipulated date and time. This kind of treatment may be appropriate for news announcements of dramatic significance but it does seem a rather ludicrous way of trying to get some relatively minor bit of information printed. Although the 'release' is a method with a long tradition, there is something to be said for

PRESS INFORMATION
From the Theatre Royal, Bury St Edmunds

TWELFTH NIGHT

Following their very successful production of Shakespeare's
"Merchant of Venice" at Bury last autumn, VANESSA FORD
PRODUCTIONS return for the week commencing Tuesday, 22nd
September, with TWELFTH NIGHT.

This visit to Bury will be the opening week of a tour which
will take in many of the major theatres up and down the
country.

Vanessa Ford takes pride in presenting Shakespeare in the
classic tradition, free of gimmicks and laying great emphasis
on the importance of the text and on clarity of verse-speaking,
but doing this without losing any of the essential sense of
humour and fun inherent in what is arguably Shakespeare's
greatest comedy.

The performance is directed by Derek Griffiths with scenery
and lighting by Graham Walne and costumes by Tim Goodchild.

The company includes Graham Ashe, Ben Bazell, Tracy Booth,
Anthony Calf, John Dallimore, Jane Danielle, Sarah Finch,
Charles Jamieson, William Lawford, Antony Simons and John
Waldon. A number of local children, who were selected by
audition earlier this summer will be playing the smaller parts.

TUESDAY, 22nd SEPTEMBER to SATURDAY, 26th   Nightly at 7.30 pm

Matinees : Wednesday & Thursday at 1.30
           Saturday at 2.30

NB. The Company are expected to be Dress Rehearsing in the
     Theatre on Monday 21st September and I anticipate that
     it will be possible to make arrangements for press to
     take photographs if they wish.

FRANCIS REID will be delighted to answer any queries on (0284) 5127
Westgate Street, Bury St Edmunds, IP33 1QR

A routine press release distributed to a mailing list of local newspapers, radio and
TV stations. A few, known to have a reasonable amount of regular theatre space
also received a second sheet giving actor biographies. Auditions for local children
had generated considerable previous press and television coverage.

PRESS INFORMATION
From the Theatre Royal, Bury St Edmunds

SPECIAL OXBRIDGE OFFER

"ATTEND BOTH UNIVERSITIES IN THE SAME WEEK AND GET 50P OFF EACH!"

That's the midsummer offer from Bury's Theatre Royal

For Monday & Tuesday (June 30th & July Ist) <u>Oxford Revue Group</u>
bring their 1980 Revue "RADIO ACTIVE".

Then for the remainder of the week (wednesday July 2nd onwards)
<u>Cambridge Footlights</u> present "ELECTRIC VOODOO".

Oxbridge Revues have been a major source of star talent in the past.
Here is a chance to see what the future holds.

Who needs a boat race?

£1, £1.75, £2.50 <u>and</u> there's 50p off each ticket if you book for
both of these shows at the same time!

<u>AND</u> , *as a special bonus in these enlightened times,*

history is made!!

FOR THE FIRST TIME EVER, this year's Footlights Revue cast
includes more women than men!

WHICH UNIVERSITY will set the entertainment trend of the 80s ???

OXFORD'S "Radio Active" (Britain's First National Local Radio Station)
<u>OR</u>
CAMBRIDGE'S "Electric Voodoo" (A look at the end of the world,
                                      Busby Berkley Style)

only at Bury Theatre Royal - <u>week commencing June 30th.</u>

FRANCIS REID will be delighted to answer any queries on (0284) 5127
Westgate Street, Bury St Edmunds, IP33 1QR

Routine press release gave the details of each of these student revues, but this
extra sheet offered several 'angles'.

heading one's announcements with the less dramatic but more accurate 'press information'. Whatever the heading, it is important to adopt a recognisable house style so that a reporter can easily locate theatre news when hunting amongst the avalanche of paper that daily descends on any newsdesk.

Any such information sheet should be geared, particularly on matters of detail, to the needs of its specific recipient. But the opening paragraph must always be a short, clear, concise summary of the facts that represent the claim for the information to be regarded as news.

Newspapers

There are three types of newspapers available to most theatres: dailies, weeklies and free sheets. Most national dailies are concerned only with West End theatres on a regular basis, although the *Guardian* has a policy of reviewing different regional productions on virtually a daily basis, and including regional productions in theatre news and features coverage. A regional theatre with a possible national story might circulate a short statement in the hope of exciting interest: no need for details, the reporter would flesh out the story from a telephone interview.

Whether to release news generally or give it as an exclusive is always a tricky decision. Items for gossip writers' diaries need to be exclusive. And tales of success or distress are more likely to be considered news, and treated as such, if they are exclusive. A theatre dependent on two or three local papers just has to share its news around. Often this is easy: differences in editorial policy and emphasis indicate categories. In particular dailies and weeklies have different attitudes to theatre coverage. And you can play discreet games with deadlines: like releasing just after a weekly has gone to press so that the daily has an exclusive. Or encouraging a daily to print by releasing just before a weekly's deadline, in the hope that the daily will wish to steal 24 hours on its rival. These games work best with keen young apprentice journalists.

There is little point in calling press conferences unless you have a really dramatic announcement that must be told to everyone at exactly the same time, or you wish to make a splash at the announcement of a new season. Whenever possible, journalists do not want to hear the same story: give them basic information on paper and elaborate in conversation. The best reason for a theatre press conference is to produce a newsworthy person like an author or actor when such a person is hitting town for only one day — if they are around longer, consider individual interviews. Lay on refreshments with alcohol options and ensure that each journalist gets a solo chat with the celebrity to flesh out the circulated biographical details.

There are really two categories of theatre editorial coverage: intermittent news items and regular input to entertainment feature pages. Most local dailies have a weekly arts and entertainment feature on a fixed day, and every weekly has an entertainment round-up. The weeklies are particularly strong in that the editorial matter usually shares pages with the entertainment adverts. They come out just before the weekend and combine a hard look at the weekend outing options with a preview of the week ahead. They usually have a fixed space for the local theatre and there is every possibility of a regular picture slot.

   Information sent to a weekly should include lots of biographical back-up to the main facts. The photographs need to be supplied by the theatre unless a production theatre can offer facilities to the paper's own photographer — rehearsal shots for the first week, production shots thereafter. Picture editors tend to prefer a group action shot from the production rather than a mug shot of the star. And whatever the philosophy, the plain fact of life is that picture editors prefer girls, they prefer glamorous girls, and they prefer girls who have got it and flaunt it.

Photo calls

Proper photo calls are difficult to slot into the dress rehearsal schedule but they are essential for publicity. The theatre requires production photographs for display and general purpose publicity, while some newspapers will wish an opportunity to take their own pictures. Most production photographs are now taken as action shots during the run of a dress rehearsal but wise theatres try to provide a short call for the press to take posed pictures. For convenience of costume and make-up, the best time is immediately prior to a dress rehearsal. The length of the call will vary from half-an-hour to an hour or so, depending upon the size and type of production and the number of photographers. Having made a call and informed the press, it is absolutely essential to be ready at the stipulated time. Production schedules inevitably slip, but photocalls must be considered sacrosanct. A short list of significant moments from the play should be prepared: moments selected to combine significance with strong visual interest, rotating the actors in two and three-shot combinations. If these moments are identified as lines in the script, the cast can slip in to them easily. The director should control the call, rough positioning the actors then letting the photographer arrange the final pose. The theatre's press officer should be on hand to ease tensions, generally lubricate and help with the spelling of names.

Free sheets

A recent and apparently expanding development in the newspaper world are the local free newspapers distributed without charge to every household within a defined area. Their purpose and content is advertising, with only

a limited amount of supportive editorial which is put together by the advertising staff who welcome copy and are not averse to saying so when they
solicit advertising. Indeed they are the one possible exception to the rule that
editorial information should never be enclosed in the same envelope as
advertising copy. Free sheets often print material exactly as submitted and
can be a very positive way of reaching potential new audiences.

Magazines

Monthly magazines obviously require more general material, mainly of the
image-building type. Their time scales make them unsuitable information
dispensers except for the most basic seasonal stuff. However most counties
have illustrated magazines which run entertainment features in certain
issues prior to 'entertainment seasons', particularly Christmas. These magazines tend to be strong in dining out columns which are a good way to try
to promote the theatre's catering, always providing that the cuisine will
stand the scrutiny of some of the rather purple prosed palates who contribute
these articles. Some of the magazines are more interested in who attends the
theatre than in the performances they watch. This will be reflected in the
photographs they publish. Swallow your artistic heckles, this can be good
image stuff. It will not put off that young, informal and committed audience
that you are trying to build: they don't read the county glossies. Profiles of
theatre personalities are possible and picture features of the backstage mys-
teries are regular repeaters. Do not forget the Sunday supplements. Send in
seasonal press releases, brochures and throwaways. It can be a very pleasant
surprise to find your panto poster in a Christmas Eve montage.

Television

The main hope for television coverage is the regional magazine programmes
that follow the early evening news. Studio interviews are the simplest and
cheapest, particularly if the studios are in the same town as the theatre. But
it can be difficult to get an actor to a studio seventy miles away during final
rehearsals. Moreover an interview recorded in a theatre with clips of the
show and backstage activity (probably including the inevitable making-up
shots in the dressing room) not only is better for television's 'out and about'
news image, but is an infinitely more positive exposure for the theatre.

The theatre must be prepared to cooperate fully in providing facilities
and adjusting to the TV crew's schedule. Shooting TV news items has
become simpler over the years, first with a reduction in the weight of lighting
equipment and now with the swing from film to video recording using ENG
(Electronic News Gathering) techniques. Theatre union agreements normally allow the filming of short extracts for promotion without extra pen-

alty payments. Getting a three minute item can take up a lot of the day. But just think what the cost of buying that free peak time would be!

Television does not cover theatre as a matter of routine informative news. They need an 'angle'. Television personality playing an unaccustomed role is a favourite, as is the opening of a summer season, or local boy makes good. And all the media love a threat of closure — success is considered boring in a disaster prone world. From time to time there is a possibility of a feature on the theatre itself rather than a specific production or personality: anniversaries, appeals in aid of extensions, reopening after modernisation etc. can provide a motive.

Getting TV slots is mainly a matter of keeping them informed. Match TV faces to their own channel. And if one channel has decided to cover an event and the 'other side' rings up, do come clean and tell them immediately that the opposition is coming.

Radio

Recent years have seen the build up of a network of local radio stations, each of which can only be heard in a relatively small geographical area. Their programmes have a mostly local content, strong in community news and listings of entertainment events. Getting into their 'What's On' programmes is a simple matter of identifying the right programme presenters and sending them regular information. It is usually worthwhile sending to several presenters, including those who have shown a tendency to slot entertainment items into record programmes. Weekly specialist record programmes like jazz, country, rock, ,folk, etc. each have a committed core audience who are a definable target for a theatre's programme in their areas of specialist musical interest. There is usually no difficulty in getting a concert plugged and the artist's record played. Even the newest groups have cut some sort of disc as part of their bid for fame and to sell after their concerts, as much as a status symbol as for revenue. Local radio stations do not have record libraries quite as extensive as one might expect: get them a copy.

Some shows, including plays, are now preparing tapes as part of their promotion package and this practice could and surely should grow with the continuing development of the local radio network, particularly as it moves into areas of thin population where the potential advertising revenues will restrict their operation to a very tight budget indeed.

No local radio station has much of a budget for paying anyone other than its presenters. So local radio and local theatre have a considerable degree of mutual dependence: the theatre needs exposure and the radio station needs free stars. For a theatre, especially a touring theatre, to be able to pop a 'name' into the studio for a five minute interview is beneficial to both sides. It is relatively quick and painless. Time and personnel in local radio are so stretched that there is rarely time to go out to record then edit for transmission. Much of the appeal of the medium is based on its informality and more and more theatre people are getting used to going into a studio in the middle of a programme, having a quick chat with the presenter during the record and then doing a live interview straight off, possibly with another record in the middle for a breather.

And if getting to the studio is impossible, then there is always the telephone. It is useful to establish with a touring company if anyone is prepared to be interviewed on a phone-in from the previous week's touring theatre. Pass the name and number to the radio station. There is a lot of free airtime waiting for a theatre prepared to do a little work.

Talks

Any community has many societies and clubs with a programme to fill. A talk about how their local theatre works is always a welcome programme filler. This presents a twofold opportunity. Firstly to do some promotional work, soft-selling not only to individuals but to the club who will frequently decide to have a follow up in the form of a party booking (make sure they are recognised and welcomed on arrival). And secondly to explain the strange economics of theatre: this can be of particular value when addressing organisations such as Rotary, Round Table, etc.

Talks to young people, particularly if they can be held in the theatre, can almost be classified as essential. It is amazing how many school leavers do not know what happens in their theatre, or only associate it with outings to Shakespeare and pantomime. The liberal and community studies classes of Further Education Colleges are always interested in such talks and indeed often request them. A talk to day-release students can be particularly rewarding. When talking to young people it can be helpful to explain the process of visiting a theatre and buying a ticket: a slide sequence can remove the mystery of ritual which can frighten some people off from making their first theatre visit. Always have lots of literature to distribute: some will find its way home to parents.

Print

Theatres use a lot of printed paper to inform and promote. In production theatres all this will be the theatre's own responsibility, whereas in touring theatres its provision will be a matter determined by contract. It is an obvious economy for all print for a weekly tour to be produced at one time from a uniform design to which local details known as 'tops' can be added. The detailed wording of these tops forms part of a printing requisition sent by the resident theatre management to the touring manager, listing the numbers required for each size and type of poster, leaflet, etc. One night stands rarely supply more than a token quantity of print but extra can usually be bought at cost: this is normally in the form of posters with a blank area for local overprinting or hand signwriting of details. For tours of several one night stands coordinated by a Regional Arts Association, it is useful to have a common leaflet listing all the venues with details of dates, times and prices.

There are two main types of printed matter: that informing of the total programme on a day-by-day basis and that promoting individual items or series of items within that programme.

Posters

The largest poster sites available to most theatres in sufficient numbers to warrant printing, even by the small run silk screen process is Double Crown (20 × 30 inches). Anything larger is likely to be a one-off with special dimensions best dealt with by signwriting. The bulk of postering is done with a size of around 10 × 15 inches which is variously called hanging card, display card, or more traditionally, box office card. The word 'card' indicates its function as a poster that can easily be hung in shops, hotel foyers, etc.

An ideal poster should stimulate a passerby to stop, then cross the road to read the details. The image and typography of a poster promoting a specific production should indicate the content and style of that particular production. A theatre's day-by-day listing summary poster needs clarity of typography and a consistent positive style recognisable to the regular audience. It will carry the theatre's distinctive logo and there is much to be said for including a picture of the theatre as a guide to visitors and a possible stimulus to that majority of the population who never step inside a theatre.

A problem that has been touched on is the increasing number of production credits to be included by contractual requirement. Whoever heard of a lighting or sound designer's name selling seats? Well, regular theatregoers do begin to recognise names and the involvement of a known production team can often bolster up the possibility of these regulars taking a chance on whether or not a new producer is likely to be presenting a piece to high standards. Indeed the design team are more likely to be known than many of the small part actors. One has to realise how necessary it is for everyone in theatre business, especially freelances, to make themselves known in a world where survival is dependent on the opportunity to practice one's craft. Before the days of standard contracts, it was common to offer good billing and a programme biography as an inducement to a minimum fee.

Leaflets

'Throwaways' is one traditional name for small leaflets, 'handbills' is another. These names convey the purpose and form of most leaflets. They

Theatre Royal
Bury St Edmunds

Box Office Telephone 5469

Administrator & Licensee:
Francis Reid

Saturday 19th September at 5 pm & 8 pm   *£3.00 to £5.00*

THE PRESERVATION HALL JAZZ BAND
from New Orleans

Sunday 20th September at 5.30 pm & 8.30 pm   *£2.50 & £3.00*

COUNTRY & WESTERN
with Berni Flint & Chubby Oates

Tuesday 22nd to Saturday 26th September at 7.30 pm   *£1.50 to £3.50*
Matinees on Wednesday & Thursday at 1.30 and Saturday at 2.30   *(Matinees: £2.00)*

TWELFTH NIGHT

Week Commencing Monday 28th September   *£1.50 to £3.50*
Monday to Friday at 7.30 pm Saturday at 5 pm & 8 pm; Thursday at 2.30 pm   *(Matinees: £2.00)*

THE AXE'S EDGE
Peter Adamson *(Len Fairclough* of Coronation Street) stars in his own play

---

Tuesday 6th to Saturday 10th October.   *80p to £1.25*
Mornings & afternoons (times vary)

THE PLAYBOARD PUPPETS
In *"A Waddle and a Quack"*

Sunday 11th October at 7.30 pm   *£1.75 to £3.25*

HEARTSONG
A Charity Gala in aid of the British Heart Foundation

Week Commencing Monday 12th October   *£1.50 to £3.50*
Monday to Friday at 7.30 pm   *(Matinees: £2.00)*
Saturday at 5 pm & 8 pm; Thursday at 2.30 pm

HIGH INFIDELITY
a sparkling comedy with Aimi Macdonald

Sunday 18th October at 5.30 & 8.30 pm   *£2.00 to £4.00*

COUNTRY & WESTERN
with Frank Ifield & Jimmy Lawton

Monday 19th October at 7.30 pm   *£1.00 to £3.00*

THE WHEELTAPPERS & SHUNTERS SHOW
with Colin Crompton and full company

Tuesday 20th October at 7.30 pm   *£1.25 to £2.75*

RACHEL MASTERS *(Harp)* & PAUL EDMUND-DAVIES *(Flute)*

Wednesday 21st October at 7.30 pm   *£3.00 to £5.00*

TOM PAXTON

**For details of ticket prices, party booking concessions, transport
subsidies, and student standby bargains, please call 5469.**

Printed by Miro Press, Bury St. Edmunds

A National Trust Property

Composite poster for the month's programme in a mixed programme theatre — giving what, when and how much. Paper colour changing monthly (this was black type on yellow paper).

Malcolm Knight presents

TREVOR BANNISTER

From TV's "Are You Being Served?"

CAROLYN JONES

From TV's "Crossroads"

in

CHARLES DYER'S

Rattle of a Simple Man

ROGER FOX

Directed by
CHARLES SAVAGE

Settings designed by
JAMES HELPS

THEATRE ROYAL — Bury St. Edmunds

Box Office Tel. (0284) 5469

Administrator and Licensee: Francis Reid

Week Commencing Monday, 25th February

Nightly at 7.30

Seat Prices: £1.50, £2, £2.50, £3   Monday only: Two seats for the price of one.   20o/o reduction for Parties
of 10 or more from Tues. to Fri. inclusive.   Student Standby: unsold seats to bona fide students at 7.15pm

Produced in three sizes (double crown poster, box-office card and throwaway leaflet) the artwork carries different 'tops' (in this case printed at the bottom) for each theatre on the tour. Printed black on white paper with a second colour (red) used sparingly but forcefully for the play title and the stripes on the scarf. The drawing conveys something of the content of the play while the photographs and captions identify the stars and associate them with their television roles.

are miniature posters placed in positions where they can be picked up (often on impulse and subsequently thrown away) or included as part of a mailing. Size is around A5 but proportional to the poster since contemporary printing techniques make it easy to produce them from the same artwork as the posters. Extra information may be printed on the reverse, including a postal booking form if required. The rate at which leaflets are picked up is a measure of their appeal and consequently also some indication of the effectiveness of the poster that they copy.

Brochures

The core of a theatre's information is the folded diary of events brochure listing every event in a seasonal period with full details of every show for perhaps the next two or three months or so, and a brief summary look ahead to some of the events beyond that point. The actual length covered varies with type of theatre: a regional rep diary can obviously cover a longer period than a mixed programme theatre with a high proportion of one nighters. In addition to standard information like dates, times and prices, each production has a condensed promotional message indicating something of the nature of its content. The diary will also include sundry information — especially booking procedures, discounts, etc. It is heavily informative but with promotional overtones. The key to the comprehensive nature of a good theatre diary brochure lies in the fact that not only the public but the theatre staff will consult it to see what's on.

For subscription series it is customary to produce additional brochures which are heavily promotional to the point of hard sell. Other brochures to be found include promotional ones, with membership forms, for playgoer's clubs. And images can be assisted with potted histories of the theatre's illustrious past — possibly advertising the fuller account which every theatre that has come of age should endeavour to publish.

Badges and stickers

Car stickers carry the message free and they carry it far and wide: worth giving them away. Badges with messages such as 'I saw Aladdin at the Theatre Royal' do the same thing: people even buy them!

In house magazines

An extension of the advertising free sheet type of local newspaper has been experiments in producing theatre magazines in newspaper format. Content includes a diary of events and supportive articles on forthcoming productions and personalities associated with the theatre. Support comes from advertising — partly by space bought by the theatre itself and partly by local traders, both those who, like restaurants and taxis, benefit directly from the audience, and those who merely choose this way of supporting their local theatre.

House publication style

A theatre's print should project a consistent and recognisable image. To achieve a unity of style in layout and typography really requires a specialist design although, given a sympathetic printer, many of the creative skills lie within the theatre team. Any style will gradually lose edge and, except in the most venerable institutions, a new look is advisable every two or three years.

The most difficult problem in theatre print is to find a style which is elegant but still sufficiently jazzy to attract that enormous potential audience whose theatregoing varies from occasional to never. Sadly, in a world where the senses are besieged with advertising messages, elegance has often to give way to razzmatazz. A successful marriage between the two must be our aim — elegant informative razzmatazz.

Spreading the printed word

What do we do with all this print? Brochures and leaflets have to be placed in positions where they can be picked up: the theatre foyer, public libraries, tourist information centres, etc. And some will be mailed. Posters need sites and in theatre terms that usually means persuading people, particularly shopkeepers, to display them free. Directly controlled municipal theatres usually have access to the sort of prime sites that tend to be denied to trust theatres, even when the local authority is contributing a goodly subsidy. The polite and cheerful boy on a bicycle is probably still the best poster delivery system for the inner town but many are likely to be mailed both to general and selective lists.

Mailing

Direct mailing is an expensive but essential tool for getting information to the right people. Playgoers' Societies and Friends of the Theatre organisations normally get automatic mailing of each new events diary. If they are autonomous organisations, their committee will doubtless make a blanket contribution to theatre funds to cover the costs. Other people will ask to go on the mailing list and there has to be provision for accepting them. Often there is a charge but sending reminders and dealing with small remittances is so time consuming that there is much to be said for a free list. After all, these are people who have identified themselves as interested and taken positive steps towards getting information. Should we charge committed interested potential audience for the privilege of receiving advertising matter? If a charge is made, there is much to be said in favour of making it three yearly rather than annually. All free lists need to be cleaned up regularly and once a year there should be a simple returnable questionnaire asking whether the recipient still wishes to continue receiving mailings and if the address is still correct.

It is reasonable to ask any interested person to commit the return postage but the rules of any renewal system, paid or free, have to be simple: there is nothing quite as sad (or fierce, according to temperament) as the regular supporter who thinks that his mailing has been cut off by mistake (or malice).

There are various addressing machines available and most of them permit coding for selection of specialised sections. The best system is to capture the lists on a computer which on request will print out selective lists on peel/off stick/on adhesive labels. Computers as a management tool are creeping into theatres and we can look for an early acceleration in the use of these techniques. Meanwhile some local authority owned theatres have access to computer time and some authorities make their computers available at a token charge to the trust theatres whom they support.

Selective lists of party bookers, W.I.s, schools etc. can be built up from the yellow pages, year books, etc. and refined from box office plans. Lists of known regulars, also prepared from old plans, are particularly useful for a concentrated attack on a show with a slow moving booking pattern.

With help from the local education authority's drama advisers, information can be sent to schools through the internal mailing system. Advantages are that it arrives post free and with something of an official blessing. Disadvantage is that it may not reach the desk of a particular school's theatre enthusiast. A little questioning will soon build up a list of Drama and English teachers who deserve a personal mail shot in addition.

Displays

The theatre foyer, stairs and bars are primarily areas for selling coming attractions as are those foyer areas penetrated only by an audience who have already bought tickets for the current show and now need to be enticed to the next. The outside of a theatre has to be largely a hard sell for the current show with lots of production photographs and artist's photographs. Even if the show is sold out. It does the image no harm to turn away chance audience tonight provided that it is clear when seats are available in the future. Remember too that a theatre needs happy actors and that actors are unhappy if they consider that the front of house displays are doing their egos less than justice.

The success image

The majority of the public do not understand theatre finance. They do not appreciate that, as a result of all sorts of possible accidents of funding, a theatre may be running a deficit yet operating successfully and cost effectively. Their logic is simple. If the theatre is losing money, it must be because nobody goes. And if nobody goes, it must be because the shows are no good.

It is therefore important to avoid regular horror stories of possible closure. Sooner or later there will be a crisis: but this crisis must be prepared for by an education programme. Never talk to the press about profit and loss. Talk about operating surpluses and deficits. At best report that the theatre is operating within its budget and emphasise audience size and, if possible, audience growth.

It is difficult to interest the media in success: failure makes more interesting news. Sooner or later a theatre will find itself on the defence. But if that theatre has been honest and helpful with reporters, the ride will not be too rough. There are three cardinal rules:

* Help the media find angles
* Always be happy to provide quotes — never ever refuse to comment
* And that includes the theatre chief who must *always* be available to the press.

The success image must also be conveyed in print. But with some subtlety and sincerity if the message is to retain any credibility. While a certain amount of trumpet sounding is expected and accepted in advertising, an excess can induce a counterproductive cynicism in the people that the message is intended to impress.

Surveys

Information is a two-way process. A theatre needs to know what its audience are thinking and what they want. The traditional method has always been based on management's gut reaction plus the evidence that the box office provides as an indication of audience preferences. To collect more positive data, audience research surveys may be carried out and these provide useful data which is difficult to acquire in any other way — particularly in quantifying the value of the various forms of publicity. Surveys can also produce useful statistics to support grant applications.

10   Selling seats

If our display of information and projection of image has worked, there should be a potential audience interested in the possibility of seeing each production. Now we must make the idea of actually attending seem an attractive enough proposition for people to buy tickets. When they have made the buying decision, we need machinery to sell them a ticket, and to account for the proceeds of that sale. Thus selling seats is a twofold operation:
* Encouraging people to make a decision to buy.
* Selling them the ticket.

Selling the desire to buy

Everyone loves a bargain. Indeed, in the atmosphere of today's selling techniques, everyone expects a bargain. Now all theatre seats are a bargain since their manufacturing costs are subsidised. However the clamour of the market place has created an atmosphere in which any buyer feels inadequate if they have not beaten the system by paying less than the published 'regular' price. Indeed the problem of discounting is that anyone on a full price ticket begins to wonder if they are the only one. A situation similar to the airlines where the only full fare passengers are now those who are able to buy seats with their company shareholder's money rather than with their own.

Theatre has very few such business travellers but in many other respects there are similarities between theatres and aircraft. We have already noted that there is nothing more unsaleable than an aircraft seat after take-off or a theatre seat after curtain-up. So it is not surprising that there is a similarity between airline and theatre marketing methods. The higher regular ticket price is for those whose lives are too flexible to buy an Apex flight or subscription series, yet not flexible enough to risk a standby.

Discounts

Theatre marketing has therefore become heavily involved in promotional offers based on discounting the regular published ticket price. Discounting steers a delicate path between attracting audiences with apparent bargains, and not discouraging them with complex conditions and procedures. Various methods are described below.

Subscription series

Series booking has long been the mainstay of Central European repertoire theatres. The season's programming is built around the possibility of attending on the same day each week to catch the entire season's repertoire, or perhaps fortnightly for all the music theatre productions, or monthly for all the opera or all the operettas, etc. This helps to fulfill the educational needs that are an inherent aim of any subsidised national or regional theatre. It encourages and just as importantly ensures an audience for the works which, by being more adventurous, seem less attractive. It builds theatre-going into a regular habit and helps to make audiences of individuals. Encouragement to subscribe principally takes the form of heavy discounting, but there are strong subsidiary attractions in the simplicity of one booking action plus assured seats for the more popular shows in what are generally heavily booked theatres.

There has always been series selling in Britain but it is only recently that it has become fashionable. Subscription schemes were possible and

A GREAT OPPORTUNITY TO SAVE MONEY AND ENJOY SUPERB, LIVE THEATRE AT ITS BEST!

- Book for all 7 plays and see 2 FREE!

- Enjoy excellent theatre at a price you can afford — Season Ticket Holders save up to 30% on normal box office prices!

- Book for all 7 plays and get your PROGRAMME for each play FREE!

- With our VOUCHER SCHEME you don't have to choose your dates now you can decide nearer the time.

- Book your dates before September 4th — and choose your seats as well!

- Parking is easy — There's a large cheap car park opposite the theatre.

- Enjoy a reasonably priced meal from our SUPERB BUFFET and meet your friends in our THEATRE BARS.

- A whole season's theatre-going for only £20!

- Guard against price increases

∗ SO LONG AS YOU EXCHANGE YOUR VOUCHERS AT LEAST 4 WEEKS BEFORE THE PERFORMANCE OF YOUR CHOICE.

Over recent seasons, largely because we now announce almost a whole year's theatre-going of seven plays in advance, it has often happened that several productions were virtually sold out even before opening night.

For instance, last season, THE SCHOOL FOR SCANDAL at Christmas, then Ayckbourn's SEASON'S GREETINGS and Noël Coward's DESIGN FOR LIVING were so heavily booked that many unlucky people had to miss the productions. Indeed, SEASON'S GREETINGS, ANOTHER COUNTRY and DESIGN FOR LIVING were all so popular that they subsequently transferred to the West End, where, of course, theatre-goers had to pay West End prices.

Peter Vaughan, Brian Hall and Gareth Hunt in last season's Alan Ayckbourn success 'Season's Greetings'.

But our SEASON TICKET HOLDERS weren't disappointed and were able to see ALL the productions. They also avoided any frustrating queuing for tickets and paid MUCH LESS than normal box office prices for their tickets. So why don't YOU become one of our valued season ticket holders this year? It couldn't be simpler. Once you've returned your booking form, your PRIORITY BOOKINGS are GUARANTEED.∗

CHOOSE FROM 2 SCHEMES

SCHEME A

SEE 7 FINE PLAYS FOR THE PRICE OF 5

SEE ALL 7 PLAYS IN OUR SEASON — BUT ONLY PAY FOR 5 No matter when you choose to come — or wherever you choose to sit — you always make a saving of almost 30% on our normal box office prices with this scheme. That means that you can save up to £11 per person! Come during the week, and you can see all 7 plays in our season for only £20! And remember, Season Ticket Holders who book 7 plays for the price of 5, get their programme for each production FREE.

SCHEME B

SELECT 4 PLAYS FROM OUR SEASON — BUT ONLY PAY FOR 3 Under scheme B you always make a saving of 25% on our normal box office prices. So you can save up to £5.50 per person. Come and see the 4 plays of your choice during the week and it can cost as little as £12!

Subscription selling: part of a Greenwich Theatre seasonal colour leaflet.

inevitable once marketing personnel were appointed to implement them. A catalyst was required to trigger off the torrent, and that catalyst appeared in the late 1970s in the shape of one Danny Newman who had successfully launched subscription selling in a number of North American venues and written a book called *Subscribe Now!* The single exclamation mark in the title is surprising in view of the evangelical zeal with which Mr Newman pursued his crusade. Through the book, through seminars and through the resulting press coverage, theatre managers were made to feel guilty about their apparent lack of dynamism in filling empty seats. However salvation was offered through dynamic subscription selling. Even *Stage* newspaper, that bastion of moderation and objective reporting, got sufficiently carried away to run a leader entitled 'Empty Seats an Affront to Theatre Managers'.

Subscription selling is relatively easy to organise in producing theatres where all productions are under one management's control and where total advance planning is possible. A mixed programme theatre has problems because the productions originate from a series of different sources, often at rather short notice. However some subscription schemes, particularly those working on vouchers, can cope with a wide range of variables. The essential selling message is *five for the price of four* and variations thereon.

The subscription evangelists see an ideal world in which the single ticket buyer is virtually eliminated. Those more concerned with the totality of theatre experience welcome the audience contribution of the impulse ticket buyer. There is a lot to be said in favour of a system which sells heavily on subscription but keeps a goodly proportion for selling two weeks or so ahead, plus a small quantity for sale on the day of performance. Subscription has many advantages, not the least being the smoothing out of peaks in the pattern of seat occupancy and the generation of cash flow.

Parties

It is standard practice to allow discounts for party bookings of a minimum number, usually ten or twenty. Saturday evening is often exempted from this offer. A 10% reduction is common although this is occasionally marketed as one free seat for every ten bought. Advertised party reductions may rise to 20% or organisers may just be invited to contact the box office or party bookings department for details of special discounts. This leaves the way free for flexible selling according to the state of business. Although party booking organisers will approach the box office from time to time, this really is more of an area for positive selling using circulars, telephones and considerable flexibility in negotiating actual rates. Where the theatre has appropriate catering facilities, parties can be offered a block price for an evening out. And social nights can be constructed on the lines of 'Come to the theatre on the same night as the county's other W.I. branches — meet each other, and the actors, in the bar afterwards.' Some Regional Arts Associations run subsidised transport schemes covering up to 50% of a party's travel costs, but many of these schemes have been disbanded or diluted, apparently under pressure from the central Arts Council. It is important to remember that many organisations plan their programmes of events and outings several months ahead.

School parties

Special terms may be offered to school parties — both for ordinary performances and for special matinees arranged at times in the mornings or afternoons to suit local preferences. Many teachers prefer older children to attend ordinary theatre performances rather than special school performances: this is particularly true of plays forming prescribed examination texts. From the theatre's point of view, this makes good sense in terms of building future audiences. Performances for the youngest children tend to be given during the day, playing 'under' a different evening production. The simplest way to sell to schools is at a flat rate per head with teacher's free. Parties can then be distributed around the house to integrate with the rest of the audience at normal performances, or given first come first served seating at special matinees to encourage early advance booking. Schools need lots of advance warning, particularly around holiday times, and the selling letter should be positive in describing the proposed style of production. For non-classics, a preparatory work sheet for teachers can help to persuade a doubtful headmaster of the educational value. Some theatre companies offer discussion sessions and workshops in conjunction with schools performances.

Playgoers Societies

Autonomous supporters clubs exist basically to support: that is, to give rather than to receive. However, in recognition of their special relationship with the theatre, members are often given a period of priority booking. When price concessions are given, it is usually on particular nights, often first nights, to encourage members to come at the same time to meet each other and the cast. A few theatres run theatre clubs as a marketing tool — these are clubs without constitution or committee which have been set up specifically to offer concessions in exchange for an annual subscription. They have a period of priority booking, often a hot-line telephone number to the box office, and are mailed with special offers from time to time. The publicity may even be in the form of 'join for £X and save £Y'.

Friends
Organisations:
part of a Scottish Opera
Friends
recruiting leaflet listing
membership
benefits.

Pensioners

Discounts for those of pensionable age are common, especially at matinees
and perhaps weekday evenings. Such concessions should be simple: flat rate
for best available seats rather than percentage discounts. On humanitarian
grounds, they should be available in advance, not sold as standbys.

Twofers

Two seats for the price of one is a well established selling tool. On Broadway
it takes the form of vouchers distributed with varying degrees of discretion
to prop up audience figures in the later weeks of a long run. In Britain it
tends to be a published device to get an audience early on in a run, particularly at previews or first nights in regional theatres, or Monday nights on
tour, in order to get word-of-mouth comment underway. Twofers may be

offered as a concession restricted to supporters' clubs. Although called two-for-one, it is customary to treat seats as half price when selling singles and odd-numbered groups. There are really two alternative selling options for a first night: twofers or gala.

Standbys

When the performance starts, any unsold seats become valueless. It is therefore worthwhile selling them off cheaply, perhaps in the last 15 minutes prior to curtain up. Standby tickets can be sold to everyone or to specific categories. A general standby system is only suitable for a theatre with a consistently high seat occupancy because, obviously, if there is a good chance of getting a cheap standby seat, advance bookings will drop and the theatre's financial capacity will suffer. Standbys are therefore usually restricted, with the most common category being students, although in the current economic climate many theatres have opened this concession to the unemployed.

Apex

An airline discounting category which theatres have not yet explored to any great extent, other than in connection with subscription series, is advance purchase . . . i.e. any seats bought more than, say, three weeks prior to opening would be subject to, say, 10% discount. Pushing advance sales is, remember, good for cash flow.

Comps

The success of all productions, but particularly comedies, is dependent upon a reasonably full house. From time to time there are circumstances when it is impossible to get a decent house without giving away seats. This has to be done with the utmost discretion and the smaller the town, the more discreetly must the house be 'papered'. Nurses are the most acceptable traditional category with police as runners up, and no eyebrows are raised if theatre staff have seats to give away to friends from time to time. Complimentary seats are also traditionally used to lubricate a theatre's relationships with people who display posters, and with people who lend furniture, etc., or give discounts. Alas if a show will not sell, it also often proves difficult to give away seats!

Selling the ticket

Having reached the decision to buy, each member of the potential audience needs to be sold a ticket for a seat. Alas, in too many theatres this can still be something of an obstacle race, requiring such a degree of patience and persistence that it can take some considerable determination to follow through the decision to buy. The problem is a historical one arising mainly from poor status and working conditions awarded to box office staff who are the major point of contact between a theatre and its audience. However matters are improving and if the new technology is used properly the process of ticket buying should become smoother. (It is not enough for only the ticket *selling* to become smoother.)

The box office window

Whether the box office operates traditional paper plans or has a computer, the point of sale is either a window or a telephone. For security, there is often a preference for some sort of glass barrier between seller and buyer, although modern box office design tries to provide for more personal contact than was possible through some of the tiny windows in the heavy, ornately carved box offices of the past. Open box offices can be used, including a simple counter. However, in addition to security, these do have a problem in that a surprisingly large minority of the public become rather strange and excited when they approach a box office. They wave their arms, grab things like tickets and plans, and even show frightening signs of minor aggression. It is hardly surprising that many box office clerks rapidly become cynical, even defensive. The good ones learn to suffer fools gladly and they keep reminding themselves that whereas a pair of seats represents an infinitesimally small fraction of the box office take, it is probably a major outlay for the customer. Management attention to simple things like ventilation and adequate breaks help to make a shift on the window more tolerable.

The employment of box office staff is subject to agreements between NATTKE, TMA and SWET. These agreements provide for minimum salaries, hours, overtime, holidays and sickness payments.

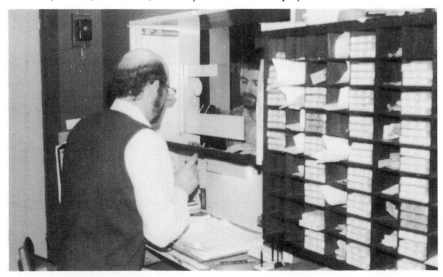

Traditional box office with racks of ticket books and sheaf of plans.

Plans and tickets

The basis of all box office operations is a seating plan for each performance plus a set of tickets bound in book form. The plan may show the exact disposition of the seats as they are in the auditorium, or it may be a more diagrammatic form. The essentials are clear row letters and seat numbers. The tickets show date, time, section of house, row letter and seat number. If there are two performances on one day, it is customary to overprint with a large 'M' or '1st' or '2nd'. Paper colour is used to help identify parts of house such as stalls/circle or left/right. The price may be printed but is frequently added at the time of sale to allow the price bands to be adjusted according to the amount of business.

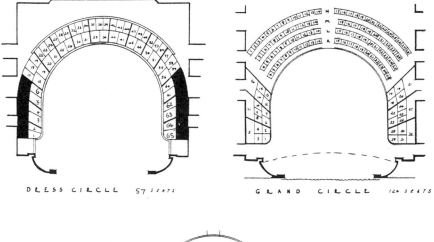

DRESS CIRCLE   57 SEATS   GRAND CIRCLE   124 SEATS

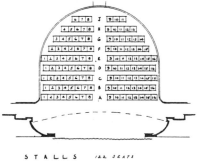

STALLS   122 SEATS

A geographical plan is the easiest for the customers to understand. However, particularly in old theatres with several circles a diagrammatic plan, *see overleaf*, may be easier for marking sales by the box office staff.

£1·50

49 48 47 46 45 44 43 42 41

1 2 3 4 5 6 7 8 9 10 11 12 13 14 15

DRESS CIRCLE RIGHT

Webster 5111 £2 5 6 14 16 17 18 19 £3 20 Homan 2578 21 22 23 24

CENTRE DRESS CIRCLE

25 N.T. 26 Blackworth 27 28 29 30 31 32 33 34 £4 35 Wills 36 7942. 37 F.R. 38 39 40 41

1 2 3 4 5 6 7 8 Handwick W.I. 24 x 270 £64·60.

I 2 3 4 5 6 7 8 B.S.F. 4578 Jones 7212 →

I 2 3 4 5 6 7 8 Burton Hero 7.15.

2 3 4 5 6 7 8 Watson W-water 2947

3 4 5 6 7 8 Erskine

A B 9 Wilson B.S.F. C D 9 Burton 378 E 9 IPS 5876 CAMB 2438 F 9 King WESTGATE G

9 10 11 12 13 14 15 16

10 11 12 13 14 15 16

9 10 11 12 13 14 15 16

9 10 11 12 13 14 15 16

9 10 11 12 13 14 15

9 10 11 12 13 14

£3

£4

GRAND CIRCLE BOXES RIGHT

Thurber (under) 2 3 4 5 £2 6 7 8 9 10 11 12 13 14 15 16 £3

THE POTATO ORCHARD

40 39 48 37 36 35 34 33 32 31 30

16 17 18 19 20 21 22 23 24 25 26 27 28 29

DRESS CIRCLE LEFT   Jones
52 2164-9   E.A.D.T.
50   55   57
53   58
51   56   59
54   £3

60
61

£2

64
63
65

Moss IPS
66 2867
67

42 Kaftal.   45 John   47   GRAND CIRCLE
43 9247   46 27876 48
44   49

STALLS

4 Don   4   1
5 6   5   2
6   6   3
7   7 Barton 4
8   8 School 5
9   9   6
10   10 ← →   7
11   11 14 @ 2.70 8
5 12   12 = /37-80 9
6 13 Arington 13 £   10
7 14   14   11
8 M.Bilp.   8   12 RED
                        13 +
                        14

Fox
2432

H   J   K   L   M   N

9   9 HOLD 15 Boggs 15 Greenwich 15 15
10 Sawing 10   16 2392 16 2867 16 16
11   11   17   17   17 Connar 17
12   11   18   18   18 IPS 18
13   19   19   19 5728 19
                   20 Thompson 20   20 20
PANTOS   21 9317 21   21 21
10%   22   22   22 22
                  23   23   23 23
                  24   24   24 24 £3
                  25   25   25 25
                                             26
GRAND CIRCLE BOXES LEFT   27
17 19   24 Mapling 28 Conar 30 28
18 20   22 W-L-W 28 7216 31
    21   23 2876 25 29   32
                  26   £2
                  27

FRIDAY FEB 22   7.30 pm.

Many box offices use a three part ticket. These tickets are only 'pulled' from the books when a sale is made. One part, known as a 'stub' is retained in the box office and the other two are given to the customer who surrenders one further part on entering the auditorium. The stubs are filed by price, either in pigeon holes or on spikes, and reconciled against till receipts at the end of each cashier's shift.

Every time a seat is allocated, an appropriate mark is made on the plan. The marks indicate the status of the seat — whether it is being held as a telephone reservation, is included in a party booking, issued as a complimentary, paid for at full rate, or at a reduced rate, etc. Procedures are not standardised: the actual markings vary from one box office to another. Most, however, use pencil to indicate a seat being held but not paid for. Coloured crayon or ink is then used when the seat is actually sold and its ticket pulled. A few use colour to indicate which cashier made the sale, but it is more common to use it to differentiate between full and reduced prices — for example, blue for full and red for reductions.

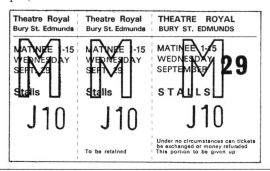

Three part ticket.

```
MARKING BOX OFFICE PLANS


Plan markings are not standardised.

The plan illustrated uses the following  marks:

    ┌──────┐
    │  23  │          in pencil  : reserved but not paid for
    │  24  │          in crayon  : paid for and ticket pulled
    └──────┘          shaded     : stubs logged in advance ledger


      ╱              ◯
     ╱   Sold as doors          Given as complimentaries

Blue crayon =  full price              Red crayon =  reduced price

Variations in other box offices include use of coloured crayons to
identify individual members of the box office staff and

    ╳   for reductions    and    ▢   for agencies
```

Markings for box office plans.

Few theatres give the customer an opportunity to see the plan. For one thing, it tends to be covered with notes as well as marks and the available seats are not at all clear to a casual untrained eye; and for another, one of the arts of the box officer is 'dressing the house' by selling seats in such a way that the auditorium looks fuller than it really is. It is however important to have a clear plan or photograph on which the suggested seats can be pointed out to the customer. Newish theatres are relatively simple: the choice is compounded of preferred price and the alternative of upstairs or downstairs. However older theatres can be tricky when they have three balconies, boxes, pillars and irregular sightlines.

The ticket selling for each performance is divided into two parts: advance and doors. The changeover point varies: it is frequently close of business on the previous day, or perhaps 6pm on that day to give time for processing the stubs before closing time. But it can be as late as noon on the day of performance or as early as 48 hours before.

The advance for each performance is calculated from the stubs. After the stubs have been reconciled with the daily takings, they are divided into parts of the theatre and subdivided into prices for each part. Each performance has a page in the advance ledger where the daily sales are entered and a running total gives the advance sales for that performance. The grand total of all the remaining performances of a particular production gives the advance sales being carried forward for that production.

At each performance, the advance sales for that performance 'mature' and a 'final return' is prepared to show the total receipts of 'matured advance' plus doors. The figures on the return are reconciled against the plan and further checks may be made against the stubs (filed stubs for the sold seats, plus stubs remaining in the book for unsold or 'open' seats).

When the ticket holder enters the auditorium, half of the two-part ticket is surrendered and may be used for a further audit check that the price shown on the face of the tickets corresponds with that on the stubs and plans. All plans and stubs are retained for a specified period which will be at least until the conclusion of the annual audit when trials will be made of plans and stubs against ledgers and returns. The books of any box office are not only open to the theatre management but also to the management of any other organisation upon whose behalf it may be selling tickets.

The performance final return is the document providing the key information on financial and numerical results. Copies are circulated to both theatre management and producing management, and it is upon these return figures that all calculations of percentages, royalties and other contractual obligations are made. Weekly summary returns are drawn up from the performance returns and these are circulated to everyone with a financial interest in the production.

PERFORMANCE RETURN

	MATURED			DOORS				
PRICE	No.	£	p	No.	£	p	FREE	OPEN
STALLS								
£ 4	55	220 — 00		11	44 — 00		2	6
£ 3	11	33 — 00		4	12 — 00			9
£ 2·70	24	64 — 80						
GRAND CIRCLE								
£ 4	23	92 — 00		6	24 — 00			5
£ 3	13	39 — 00		13	39 — 00		2	26
£ 2·70	14	37 — 80						
£ 2	12	24 — 00		3	6 — 00			7
DRESS CIRCLE								
£ 4	17	68 — 00		3	12 — 00		2	4
£ 3	7	21 — 00		1	3 — 00			11
£ 2	8	16 — 00		3	6 — 00			1
GALLERY £1·50	8	12 — 00		7	10 — 50			34
TOTALS	192	627 — 60		51	156 — 50		6	103

Performance return listing all seats sold, summarised on the 'final return', (opposite) conveniently printed on the reverse side.

FINAL RETURN

Production ___ THE POTATO ORCHARD ___ Time __ 7.30 pm.

Performance __ FRIDAY ___ FEBRUARY 22 __ 19 82

MATURED	£ 627 — 60
DOORS	156 — 50
GROSS TOTAL	784 — 10

ADVANCE CARRIED FORWARD	937 — 60

SEATS	TOTAL NO. 249
	% 71%

THEATRE ROYAL ___ BURY ST. EDMUNDS

WEEKLY RETURN

WEEK ENDING : ___ FEBRUARY 23ʳᵈ 1982

PRODUCTION : ___ THE POTATO ORCHARD

MONDAY	Matinee		
	Evening	86%	883 — 70
TUESDAY	Matinee		
	Evening	53%	468 — 00
WEDNESDAY	Matinee		
	Evening	65%	579 — 40
THURSDAY	Matinee 2.30	48%	425 — 10
	Evening	67%	720 — 80
FRIDAY	Matinee		
	Evening	71%	784 — 10
SATURDAY	Matinee 5pm	63%	590 — 00
	Evening 8pm	82%	925 — 60
	GROSS TOTAL	5376 — 70	
	VAT 15%	701 — 31	
	NETT TOTAL	£ 4675 — 39	

No. of Performances : __ 8 ___ Average % : 67%

Signed : _____ Administrator.

'Weekly return', summarising box office performance totals.

Conditions of sale

A notice should be prominently displayed at the box office reminding customers that the sale of tickets is subject to the theatre's terms and conditions
of sale. The notice will normally list these, but the essential ones may also
be included on the ticket:

* This ticket cannot be exchanged or money refunded.
* The management reserves the right to refuse admission.
* Latecomers may be asked to wait until a suitable interval.
* The use of cameras and recorders is not permitted.
* The management reserves the right to make alterations.

Agencies

Regional theatres often employ agents in adjoining towns to sell tickets
against a commission paid by the theatre. In London some tickets are sold
through agencies, traditionally known as 'libraries,' who charge a booking
fee to the customer in addition to obtaining a commission from the theatre.
Allocation of blocks of seats to agents is tricky: there is a sod's law which
ensures that the customer always wants the seat that has been allocated
elsewhere! Agencies issue their own tickets with handwritten details. It is
safer to treat these as vouchers to be exchanged for the original printed ticket
at the theatre.

   In New York and London there are ticket booths for the sale of remain-
dered tickets on the afternoon of performance. The theatres send in batches
of tickets, the number depending on the show's failure to attract a full price
audience. These are sold at half price plus a small service charge to cover
the admin expenses of the booth's operation.

Telephones

Bookings made by telephone are given a cut-off date, usually 48 or 72 hours,
up to which they will be held pending arrival of cheque. Very late bookings
are subject to collection by a stipulated time prior to curtain up. Name and
telephone number should be noted against the pencilled seats on the plan.
Only the smallest theatres, where telephones can be answered by the cashier
on the window, are able to give specific seat numbers on a telephone booking.
A separate telephonist cannot have immediate access to the plan and the
booking therefore has to be for the best available seat.

   Customers ring the box office before and after even the most extended
opening hours: it is good public relations to have an answering machine
giving the box office opening hours, details of the current show and its ticket

availability, ending with an assurance that seats may be booked on this number during normal opening hours.

In small theatres it may be useful to be able to switch in busy periods to a tape which apologises to telephone callers, saying that telephone service is temporarily suspended due to a large queue resulting from the enormous success of the current production.

Credit cards

Telephone bookings have been immensely simplified by the use of credit cards. Once the customer has given name and credit card number, the sale is immediately confirmed. The box office may then offer to add postage costs and send the tickets by mail, or to retain them for collection. Telephone credit card bookings have a lower 'floor' limit for obtaining authorisation from the card issuing company, but several transactions can be accumulated and authorisation obtained for the series on one telephone call, providing that this call is made before handing over any tickets. Credit cards are also becoming increasingly used for personal purchases at the window, although some theatres restrict their use in the hour prior to curtain up. However it is doubtful if the little time thereby saved compensates for the niggling lowering of service to the audience.

Computers

The replacement of the box office's traditional papers and pencils with computers has begun, and this is where the future lies. The situation in the box office of the 1980s is very similar to that in the lighting control rooms of the 1970s. The computer does not replace the person but removes much of the tedious labour. In the lighting box, it has enabled the operator to concentrate on the finer nuances of timing; in the ticket box it will enable the cashier to concentrate on the finer nuances of personal relations with the customer.

The major breakthrough that the computer offers is multiple access to plans. Several windows and several telephonists can all have immediate and simultaneous access to the same plan. Indeed remote sales points anywhere can be given access to the plan for any performance, can offer its unsold seats and complete a sales transaction including the printing of the ticket.

A computerised box office comprises:

* A microprocessor memory file which stores electronically the information contained on a conventional paper booking plan: dates and times of performances, row and seat numbers, prices, etc. Any transaction instantly updates the information in terms of reserved, sold, discounted, etc.

* A video terminal comprising a video display screen on which any current

Computerised box office with video terminal and ticket printer. (Ticketmaster installation at the Albery Theatre, London.)

booking plan can be viewed by selecting at the keyboard which is used to interrogate the memorised plan to select seats.

* A ticket printer to produce the ticket at the moment of sale.
* And a line printer to produce returns and all kinds of accounting and statistical reports as required.

Several video terminals can be connected to one computer and this facility can be utilised in two basic ways.

With an 'in-house' system, a theatre or theatre group has its own computer to sell tickets through sales terminals on its own premises. There can be remote selling points if desired, and systems in different theatres can be linked to sell each other's tickets.

With an 'agency' system, an independent company with a central computer sets up a network of terminals selling tickets for many different theatres and other forms of entertainment. The ticket selling points can be located in shops, travel agencies, theatre box offices, etc. Such a system is financed by a commission fee on every ticket sold.

Initial installations, being for the bigger theatres, have tended to be in-house, but with expansion to smaller regional theatres there could be a healthy logic in linking the various performing arts centres within a common catchment area. Regional Arts Associations may well have a coordinating role to perform here. However in the not-so-long term, the

Above and below:
Video terminal on which
any performance's seat
plan can be selected and
modified as tickets are
sold (B.O.C.S. System).

Ticket produced by ticket
printer (B.O.C.S.
System).

development of video information systems like Prestel and Ceefax in combination with keypads and credit cards is moving towards direct home access
to all sorts of selling operations, including theatre tickets.

All systems are secure: confidential information can only be extracted by
those with a knowledge of the access code. They also meet the requirements
of auditors: the programme cannot be tampered with to falsify returns, and
a record of each transaction is made and stored until completion at least of

```
EVENT PERFORMANCE REPORT FOR EDEMO10    23-DEC-82  09:47
       ALBERY THEATRE
ST. MARTINS LANE, LONDON.
   TELEPHONE: 01-836-3878
   DEMONSTRATION EVENT
   29-DEC-1982
   EVENING PERFORMANCE
```

LEVEL	1	2	3	4	5	6	7	TOTAL	SALE
			GROSS POTENTIAL						
	457	78	46	123	47	107	42	900	6274.60
ADULT	8.50	7.90	6.90	5.90	4.90	3.50	3.00		
J-TYPE	4.50	4.50	4.50	4.50	4.50	3.50	3.00		
G-TYPE	6.90	6.90	5.90	5.90	4.90	3.50	3.00		
K-TYPE	3.90	3.90	3.90	3.90	3.90	3.50	3.00		
L-TYPE	4.25	3.95	3.45	5.90	4.90	3.50	3.00		
M-TYPE	7.90	7.90	6.90	5.90	4.90	3.50	3.00		
V-TYPE	3.50	3.50	3.50	3.50	3.50	3.50	2.00		

```
---------------------- ADVANCE/MATURED SALES ----------------------
```

	1	2	3	4	5	6	7	TOTAL	SALE
			BOX OFFICE SALES						
ADULT	26	-6	6	-6	-3	11	31	59	296.40
J-TYPE	14	4	4	8	4	12	4	50	207.00
G-TYPE	10							10	69.00
K-TYPE	83	2	6	4	2	6	2	105	405.30
L-TYPE	184	18	8	23	6	10		249	1080.80
M-TYPE	20	8	8	16	8	18	1	79	476.00
V-TYPE	6	2	2	4	2	2		18	62.00
TOTAL	343	28	34	49	19	59	38	570	2596.50
			SECONDARY BOX OFFICE SALES						
ADULT	43			11		8		62	458.40
K-TYPE	12							12	46.80
TOTAL	55			11		8		74	505.20
			OUTLET SALES						
ADULT	23	7	-6	12	3	6	-31	14	222.90
K-TYPE	20	10	10	20	10	10		80	308.00
TOTAL	43	17	4	32	13	16	-31	94	530.90
			AGENCY SALES						
G-TYPE		15						15	103.50
TOTAL		15						15	103.50
			TOTAL SALES						
ADULT	92	1		17		25		135	977.70
J-TYPE	14	4	4	8	4	12	4	50	207.00
G-TYPE	10	15						25	172.50
K-TYPE	115	12	16	24	12	16	2	197	760.10
L-TYPE	184	18	8	23	6	10		249	1080.80
M-TYPE	20	8	8	16	8	18	1	79	476.00
V-TYPE	6	2	2	4	2	2		18	62.00
TOTAL	441	60	38	92	32	83	7	753	3736.10

A major advantage of a computerised system is the ability to print out instant reports of the state of business. This print-out (Ticketmaster System) shows potential and matured ticket sales at 9.47 a.m.

the annual audit. (This record may be kept either electronically in a secondary or 'dump' store, or it may be in the form of a print-out).

For the moment, the major benefits are improved customer service through multiple access to plans, and instantly available returns. Much is made of the potential use of the statistical print-out to monitor marketing. But it remains to see whether figures churned out in every conceivable breakdown are more helpful than the instant gut reactions that sensitive, experienced box office and theatre managers immediately get from casting an eye over the familiar plans of their theatres.

```
----------------------- TOTAL SALES FOR EVENT -----------------------
ADULT      92      1              17              25          135    977.70
J-TYPE     14      4      4       8       4       12      4    50    207.00
G-TYPE     10     15                                           25    172.50
K-TYPE    115     12     16      24      12       16      2   197    760.10
L-TYPE    184     18      8      23       6       10          249   1080.80
M-TYPE     20      8      8      16       8       18      1    79    476.00
V-TYPE      6      2      2       4       2        2           18     62.00

TOTAL     441     60     38      92      32       83      7   753   3736.10

%SALES  96.49%  76.92%  82.60%  74.79%  68.08%  77.57%  16.66%  83.66%   82.75%
```

```
********************************************************************************
          THE FOLLOWING CASH AMOUNTS REPRESENT POTENTIAL SALES ONLY
                            UNSOLD TICKETS
```

```
----------------------- UNSOLD TICKETS -----------------------
OPEN       12     15      8      26      15       24     35   135
RESERV      4                    5                              9


UNSOLD     16     15      8      31      15       24     35   144


???                3                                            3


SEATING
CAP       457     78     46     123      47      107     42   900   3736.10
```

```
=====================  DISCOUNTS  =====================
GROSS                                   3736.10
LESS: TM DISCOUNT          162.44
      C/C DISCOUNT          27.21
      LIBRARY DISCOUNT       3.60
      OUTLET DISCOUNT       18.46
      TOTAL DISCOUNTS                    211.71

LESS: VAT ADJUSTMENT ON:

      TM DISCOUNT           24.37
      C/C DISCOUNT           4.08
      LIBRARY DISCOUNT        .54
      OUTLET DISCOUNT        2.77
                                          31.76

LESS: VAT                                455.56
NET VALUE OF HOUSE                       3037.07
```

```
--------------------------- TOTALS ---------------------------
POTENTIAL NET         5456.17
WEEK TO DATE          5735.12
LAST WEEK
PERFORMANCE NUMBER       5
SIGNED:      _____
NOTES:
WEATHER      _____  ___
```

The computer equivalent of the final return for a performance. (Ticketmaster System).

11 Audience care

Build your theatre on top of a mountain, with no roads leading to it. Surround it with barbed wire, make everyone wear full evening dress, charge the earth and you'll be full.

There is more than a hint of truth in this John Christie joke. He put the spirit of it into practice and it worked. Getting hold of a ticket and making the journey to Glyndebourne does demand some considerable perseverance on the part of the audience. Now this marketing ploy would not have worked for nearly half a century if the production quality had not been so high that it hits magnificent and even superlative with a seasonal regularity, and rarely falls below excellent. And it certainly would not have worked if the audience had not been treated with anything other than care and consideration from the moment of their welcome until the final goodnight.

There are theatres over which hangs a heavy spirit of 'enter ye who dare.' This is not a consequence of architecture, although it has to be said that some buildings are infinitely more welcoming than others and that progress in this area is not as consistent as one would wish. It is largely a consequence of personal attitudes. Attitudes right down through the management structure from the top office to the cleaner's cupboard. If the administration are cheerful and courteous in their dealings with their staff, then an optimistic, smiling, caring atmosphere will permeate the theatre and embrace the audience.

We must assume that if anything can go wrong, it will. House managers must be continually on the prowl, assuming that the worst is about to happen and preventing it from doing so just in time. That is why stage managers, making the traditional transitional journey through the pass door in middle age, make such good house managers — provided that they have not become engulfed in cynicism. They have spent a lifetime anticipating such disasters as scenery falling over, fuses blowing and actors breaking legs. But they are always prepared with a remedy.

An audience have to be cared for when they visit the theatre by day to buy a ticket, to have coffee, or just to look around. And they have to be cared for when they visit a performance. The 'open all day' aspect of a theatre as a community building is being increasingly recognised, but the motivation for the existence of a theatre is the performance. Both backstage and front of house, it is towards the climax of performance that the day must build.

Performance procedures

The final countdown towards the performance starts no later than one hour before the advertised time of curtain up. At that time the duty house manager will have already made a preliminary tour of all of the audience areas checking:

* All lighting including secondary emergency lights on, with no failed lamps in areas where adequate lighting is critical for safety.

* All security chains removed from the panic bolts on exits.

* No obstacles to the exits, either in the passages leading to them, or in the street outside.

* No vehicles parked around the theatre in positions which would obstruct the emergency services.

* No loose or frayed carpets which might constitute a safety hazard.

* All furniture, props and debris cleared from any rehearsals in the front of house areas.

* Auditorium either tidied up after rehearsals, with all production desks, microphones, personal equipment etc. removed; or an indication that clearing is in progress.

* All bars, confectionery and other sales points open.

* Any cast changes posted at the box office and in a prominent foyer position.

* Anticipated curtain fall time clearly exhibited.

If there are catering facilities, some patrons will already be dining in the theatre. Early arrivals begin to trickle in and should be smiled upon and bade good evening if possible.

Ushers will be coming on duty, collecting programmes and floats ready for the opening of the house at half an hour before curtain time. Five minutes before opening time, the house manager checks the auditorium again to ensure all ready including the curtain down and curtain dressing lights on. If no house curtain is being used, and with present staging styles this is most likely, it is desirable to check with the stage manager that the setting of the stage has been completed. There used to be a rather charming custom whereby the house manager stood in the stalls, back to the orchestra rail, and called out the various parts of the house. The senior person in each person responded, usually with something that sounded like 'sir' uttered in distinctly military tones. The house manager then blew a whistle and the house was open. Today there is more likely to be a check round to see that all positions are manned, followed by something like 'OK let's go'.

Tickets are torn on entering the auditorium and this is an opportunity for a smile and a good evening. Ushers inside assist patrons to find their seats but every auditorium should be clearly marked so that some of the more adventurous and the regulars can find their own seats during that inevitable bottleneck which comes with the rush following the first bar bell. Ushers should have programmes, but in a big theatre it is useful to have a programme selling point in the foyer and a pile of programmes available at the confectionery counter. Where the programme contains a lot of background material it should also be available during the day from the box office for the benefit of theatregoers who like to do their homework before the show.

While the audience are going in, the house manager should be in the foyer looking cheerful, efficient and relaxed, welcoming regulars and other important people. The house manager will, of course, be in uniform (i.e. evening clothes) for easy recognition as one in a position of authority to receive audience queries, problems and complaints. In a touring theatre, the visiting company manager will probably also be in evidence; and such members of the theatre's administration and artistic direction as are available should also endeavour to spend some time in the foyers. It all helps to create a caring, welcoming atmosphere.

At three minutes, two minutes and one minute prior to the advertised starting time (and perhaps even earlier), the stage manager will warn the audience. Either by bells or, increasingly and possibly more humanly, with a 'Ladies and Gentlemen the curtain will rise in three minutes' etc. Habitual late starts should be discouraged but it makes sense to have an established pattern by which the stage manager does not normally start the show until telephone clearance has been received from the house manager. Whenever possible this clearance should be given at the advertised time but, if there is a queue at the box office or a coach just unloading, it makes sense to have a short hold. If this is foreseen the stage manager should be advised so that the beginners' call for the actors may be delayed. The ticket sale conditions will allow latecomers to be denied entry until at least a suitable point in the action. This is however a matter for the house manager's discretion and it may be possible to sneak them into empty rear seats until the first pause. Where latecomers are absolutely forbidden, in lyric theatres for example, it is customary to offer close circuit television.

With the performance underway, many theatres enter their most difficult front of house phase: the suppression of noise. Many, but not all, new theatre auditoria are soundproof but older theatres are very prone to the clink of programme money being counted, the clatter of coffee cups being prepared and the chatter of any voices raised above a whisper. A house manager can devote a great deal of the evening to miming the word Shhh!

Otherwise this is a time to prepare for the interval. A general tidying up is the first requirement — from the removal of debris to the replenishing of the stacks of throwaway leaflets. The bar has a major washing up session to get through before pouring the pre-ordered interval drinks. The principal selling operation of the bar is concentrated in the fifteen minutes or so of the interval. To get everyone served before they are summoned by bells for the next act is only possible if the maximum number can be coaxed into pre-ordering. Printed cards are supplied for ordering, and identifying location number allocated on handing over card with payment. Happy is the bar whose design allows long shelving for laying out numbered drinks in a bar area away from the serving counter. Another method perhaps more common in North America is to have one standard price for all alcoholic drinks and another for all soft drinks and coffee. Colour coded tickets can then be bought before the show or during the interval and are quickly exchanged for drinks. The process is speeded up still more if the beer or coke is squirted from a flexible hose into a static glass. Much quicker than taking the glass to a tap, even if rather a less elegant operation.

Ice cream trays have to be loaded and for this, as indeed for all interval preparations, a fairly precise knowledge of the interval time is required. In many theatres, if the soundproofing permits, the stage manager gives a short warning at about three minutes on the foyer bells or speakers to indicate the imminent approach of the interval.

When the first act finishes and the houselights start to fade up, but not before the houselights start, the attendants should open the doors between auditorium and foyer. At least one attendant at each level will have remained in the auditorium in case of emergencies such as an audience faint. And most theatres have Red Cross or St John Ambulance volunteers on duty. Programmes should still be on sale — either with the ice cream trays or at a sales point where the audience can be directed to. In most progressive theatres of any size there will be interval facilities for the audience to buy books, postcards, records and the sort of merchandise that was discussed earlier under the heading of income.

The house manager should be on hand to answer questions and deal with (if possible, forsee) any problems. A pay telephone should be available for audience use: several will need to check with their babysitters. And then once again it is warnings and a battle to get everyone back in. Better to go up on time rather than await a house manager's clearance; but on a full house the stage manager, hopefully with the aid of a spy hole, might be wise to give an extra minute or so before calling for houselights out.

The last act is a time for cashing up sales activities. The box office should have remained open until the interval (the first one if there are two) and during the evening will have produced the final return for the performance. In a touring theatre, the house manager will ensure that the visiting management's copy of this return reaches the touring company manager. When everything is tidied up and cashed up, it may be possible to let some of the attendants leave early in rotation: but the number on duty must never fall below the minimum specified in the theatre's licence.

At the end of the performance care must be taken to ensure that the foyers do not bear that closed down forlorn look associated with a key jangling staff concerned only with locking up. Smiles and good nights are required, with the house manager (still dressed for the part) positioned in the direct line of fire for plaudits and brickbats. All exits which assist a speedy departure of the audience will be open. However, progress is inevitably a little slow and if the publicity displays are well laid out the departing audience will be faced with enticing posters and photographs for future shows. Try a slow exit from the auditorium to the doors: if the publicity you read is for the current show, there is something wrong.

When the audience is clear, the attendants will check for lost property. Most theatres are now 'no smoking' so there is less likelihood of fire hazard. Nevertheless a fire check should still be made in the auditorium. Once the audience have departed all doors can be closed and security chains fixed and padlocked where necessary. It is now essential to check over the entire front of house area for fire hazards, particularly smouldering cigarette butts. A check should also be made in all toilets to ensure that there are no flood hazards from running taps. It is customary for the house management to secure the front of house area and for the stage management to secure the stage and dressing rooms.

Very few theatres can afford a 24 hour fireman or security officer. However the local police will check the external security during the night and use their contact number for a keyholder in emergency. A pyjama call out at 2.30 am to secure an overlooked emergency exit does wonders for a house manager's security consciousness — and if the stage manager is the one called out because of a house manager's lapse, then the house manager's education will be completed next morning.

In many theatres the bar remains open for half an hour or so after the show: whether it does so depends very much on local circumstances. If there is a demand for bar service or indeed for after show suppers, then the theatre should consider ways of providing these facilities as part of the evening out concept. If bars and catering are to remain open for any considerable time after the end of the performance, ways should be sought of making other parts of the building secure while providing a controlled path to a single exit.

Day care

The theatre's public day normally begins with the opening of the box office at 10 am. The days are gone when a linkman patrolled the foyers and opened doors: normally only the box office staff will be on continuous duty in the foyer area. However there should be a duty member of the administration available rather like an orderly officer or officer of the watch. Doing other duties in the offices but popping out into the public areas from time to time to see that all's well. And of course always ready to drop everything and deal with any problems, including visitor's queries and complaints.

It seems rather obvious to say that a theatre should be alive and welcoming all day: many are, but some alas are not. While the architecture may not be intrinsically sympathetic to a friendly exciting atmosphere, there are very few foyers that cannot be brought to life by the application of a little imagination. And if the theatre is situated centrally enough to become an all day rendezvous, it can be part of the hub of everyday life rather than just peripheral.

A welcoming caring theatre is largely a result of the staff's attitude, particularly in matters of detail. Often quite subtle detail. To quote Norwich's Dick Condon, that master of all day throbbing vitality in a theatre's foyers and bars: " . . . and I saw a notice in a theatre bar which read 'No Hot Snacks Served after 7pm.' Now surely everyone knows it should have said 'Delicious Hot Snacks Available until 7pm'."

12 Housekeeping

There are certain routine procedures that any theatre must carry out to stay in business. Many of these are legal requirements but in most cases the law is merely formalising procedures that would be required in any case to be carried out in the interests of safety, tidiness and general efficiency.

The law requires that certain licenses to operate as a theatre shall be held by a nominated responsible individual rather than by the corporate operating body. This 'licensee' is usually the theatre's administrator or general manager, but depending on a particular theatre's management structure could be the theatre manager or house manager. It can be convenient for a theatre's general operation if the responsibilities of the nominated licensee extend to overseeing other statutory requirements, particularly the making of returns of all kinds.

Theatres Act, 1968

Under the Theatres Act of 1968, all premises used for the public performance of plays require a licence issued by the local authority who is thus able to control the safety aspects of a theatre's operation. There are no national standards for theatre safety in respect of fire, construction, escape and other hazards. However most authorities base their regulations on those of the Greater London Council who are the country's most experienced licensing body.

The area of contention relates mainly to the fire retardant specifications of materials used on stage, particularly on open stages thrusting into the auditorium beyond the traditional proscenium firewall with its fire curtain. It is customary for a fire prevention officer from the local brigade to inspect the scenery for each new production coming into the theatre, including every tour. Spot checks are made by applying test flames to critical materials like gauzes, and enquiries are made about any proposed use of naked flames which are normally only permitted if they are an essential integral feature of the plot.

The arrangements for these inspections are normally the responsibility of the technical or stage manager, with the theatre's general administration only becoming involved if there is a major difficulty. It is important that the fire prevention officer has full confidence in the theatre's technical manager: if there is a problem, the performance will be allowed to proceed subject to an undertaking to fireproof any offending material. The fire officer knows that on a properly managed stage there is a diminished fire risk.

There is nothing surprising about the regulations for the conduct of the public areas of a theatre. Earlier acts imposed censorship responsibilities on the authorities, but the 1968 act allows individuals the freedom to establish their own values and to regulate their exposure to anything which they may consider distasteful by choosing not to attend. What the licensing system ensures is that the building is structurally safe and sufficiently fire retardant to allow escape in as short a time as possible through adequate attention having been given to matters like size of gangways and number of clearly indicated exits.

The sort of items that are included in the licence conditions make a useful checklist for a safety conscious administration:

* Primary Maintained Lighting, providing a safety level of lighting in all areas, corridors, stairways, etc. likely to be used by members of the public. Includes certain lights which remain on in the auditorium when the main houselighting systems are extinguished during the performance. Most authorities require that there should be a 'panic' switch enabling an attendant, in the event of an emergency, to switch on the main auditorium lighting independently of the main stage switchboard.

* Secondary Maintained Lighting, providing sufficient level of light to evacuate the audience in the event of a failure of the main electricity supply. This light is normally supplied from a set of rechargeable batteries.

* A minimum number of attendants on duty, not less than sixteen years of age and wearing distinctive dress or identification such as armbands.

* All exit signs clearly marked (with letters not less than 125 mm high) illuminated with both primary and secondary lighting.

* No exit door fixed shut other than by a panic bolt and clearly marked 'Push Bar to Open'.

* All passages, stairways, ramps, courtyards etc. to which the public have access and which lead from the auditorium to the outside, to be kept free from obstruction.

* Edges of all steps made conspicuous by paint or other means.

* Gangways not less than 1110 mm.

* Seatways (the measurement between the back of one seat and the foremost portion of the one behind — the arms in the case of a tip-up seat) not less than 300 mm.

* Seats normally secured to floor, although it may be permitted to secure them together in groups.

* Restrictions on how far seats may be from a gangway, measured either in distance or number of seats. Variations permitted if size of seatways increased.

* Specified numbers and positions approved for standees.

* Type, number and positioning of fire appliances as recommended by fire service to be maintained in proper working order and ready for immediate use.

* Instruction in use of fire fighting equipment to be given to all members of staff.

* Irrespective of any action taken, the Fire Brigade should be immediately notified of any fire, no matter how small.

Magistrates' licences

Whereas the Theatres Act covers performances of drama, musical plays, opera and ballet, there are several forms of concert and variety type entertainment which are not included in its provisions. Historically, singing, music and dancing is regarded as potentially rowdy behaviour of the type that might emanate from an unruly tavern and is controlled by various acts which have not been consolidated into a single modern piece of legislation comparable to the Theatres Act. The position varies geographically with the Greater London area having its own legislation as do a group of the Home Counties, whereas most of the rest of the country comes under various local applications of the Public Health Amendment Act of 1890.

In essence a music, singing and dancing licence contains very similar conditions to a Theatres Act straight play licence, but whereas the stage licence is usually issued by a department of the local council, the music singing and dancing licence is usually issued by the magistrates' court. Both bodies seek approval from the fire service and in addition the magistrates take police advice while the council require a report from their building surveyor. Both licences have an annual renewal procedure and need to be transferred if the theatre nominates a new licensee. On both occasions a fee is payable. The fire service usually make a formal annual inspection and also may make snap inspections from time to time without prior notice.

Liquor licences

Under the Theatres Act, it is not necessary to obtain a justice's licence to sell intoxicating liquor during normal locally permitted hours. However no extension of hours can be granted and it is necessary to apply for a special licence for each occasion on which it is desired to keep the bar open after normal local closing time. Alternatively, if a theatre wishes to sell late refreshments and drinks on a regular basis, it can apply for a justice's licence under the general liquor licensing laws.

Hygiene regulations

All bar and catering operations are subject to the hygiene regulations and may be inspected by the local authorities' environmental health inspectors at any time. If anything is amiss, they will point out verbally and confirm in writing. If their requirements have not been met by the time of a follow-up visit, prosecution may ensue. However the requirements of these regulations are pure commonsense and no theatre would wish to subject its audience to hygiene risks, quite apart from the potentially devastating damage to its image and therefore to attendances.

Health and safety

The 1974 Health and Safety at Work Act, while in no way diluting the compensation aspects of older legislation, places much more emphasis on positive preventive measures. Not only is the employer required to take positive steps to ensure so far as is practicable the health, safety and welfare of all employees, but the employee is required to take reasonable care for the health and safety of himself and others who may be affected by his acts and omissions. Under the Employers Liability (Compulsory Insurance) Act 1969, an employer is required not only to insure against liability for personal injury or disease but to display the relevant certificate of insurance.

The introduction of the 1974 legislation has led to some misunderstandings and difficulties, particularly in local authority owned theatres, during the period that the inspectors have been adjusting to some of the working practices that are imposed upon theatres by the very nature of staging requirements. Nevertheless health and safety have always tended to receive less than adequate consideration in theatres and so an improvement in standards is welcome. It is an area of the operation that requires increasing vigilance on the part of the administration, on both legal and commonsense grounds.

Contracts of employment

The engagement of most theatre employees is subject to union agreements. As we have seen, Equity agreements provide for the use of a standard contract form incorporating a schedule of the agreed conditions of employment. The NATTKE agreements, although subject to the minimum conditions in the printed agreement book, have no formal printed form of contract. Under the Contracts of Employment Act 1972, every employer must provide a written statement of conditions of employment to each employee. This contract must include:

*   The parties to the contract.
*   Date of commencement of employment.
*   Rate of remuneration or the method of calculating it.
*   Hours of work.
*   Holiday entitlement and pay.
*   Sickness pay.
*   Pension.
*   Length of notice to be given and entitlement to notice to be served.
*   Expiry date if for a fixed term.
*   Procedures for grievances.

It will be noted that most standard theatre agreements that have been discussed in earlier chapters contain these provisions.

General legislation

Obviously theatre companies are not only subject to specialist legislation: they must also conform to the general laws applicable to any company, including the responsibilities for collecting income tax, value added tax, and for making returns under the companies acts, supplying statistics to the Department of Employment etc. Theatres are subject to the general laws of the country, although there are some exemptions in areas like discrimination which cannot be totally applied to matters like casting or the advertising of auditions. However British theatre seems, rather surprisingly, to survive without a need to seek frequent advice from the legal profession — unlike the American theatre where attorneys seem to play a major role in the process of administration.

Insurance

Apart from certain compulsory insurances, there are a number of risks for which cover is optional but essential. These can be combined in a comprehensive policy for a premium which is based on an estimated annual turnover and adjusted once the final figure is known. In times of inflation it is necessary to review these sums annually. The following list includes the main areas in which theatres (buildings or companies as appropriate) normally carry insurance cover:

*   Fire.
*   Consequential loss.
*   Employer's liability.
*   Theft

* Money (including money in transit)
* Special machinery such as boilers, elevators etc.
* Public liability

It is possible to take cancellation or non-appearance insurance giving cover against financial loss arising from cancellation, postponement, curtailment or abandonment of performances through accident, illness or practically any force majeure. This is perhaps too expensive to carry on a regular basis but can be considered for special events.

Peformance licences

A reminder here that theatre housekeeping includes ensuring that licences are held for:

* Scripts and music scores being performed.

A typical PRS return. The Performing Right Society issues various types of similar forms for other situations.

C 173   10m   10/72-G

THE **PERFORMING RIGHT SOCIETY,** LTD.
An ASSOCIATION of COMPOSERS, AUTHORS and PUBLISHERS of MUSIC
29/33 BERNERS STREET, LONDON, WIP 4AA

For office use only

Name of theatre XYZ THEATRE .... | Performances from 17 JAN 1983
Address HIGH STREET, NEWTOWN, BLANKS. | to   5 FEB 1983
Nature of entertainment during the period PLAY: "FAIR RETURN"
Means of performance (e.g. orchestra, pianist, vocalist, etc.) PIANIST AND TAPE PLAYER

Note Particulars should be given on this form of ALL MUSIC, WHETHER PUBLISHED OR IN MANUSCRIPT, performed by ANY MEANS, e.g. orchestras, bands, choral singers, pianists, organists, variety artists or vocalists, or by means of gramophone records, as INCIDENTAL MUSIC or as PART OF THE ACTION of a non-musical PLAY.

Office use only	TITLE OF WORK PERFORMED	DESCRIPTION OF WORK	Duration of performance	Number of times performed	COMPOSER	ARRANGER	PUBLISHER
	'CURTAIN' AND 'INCIDENTAL' MUSIC :						
	LOVELY WAY TO SPEND AN EVENING	INSTR.	3'00"	21	McHUGH, J/ ADAMSON, H		VICTORIA MUSIC
	FLIGHT OF THE BUMBLE BEE	INSTR.	3'01"	21	RIMSKY-KORSAKOV	ARR. GALWAY, JAMES	NOVELLO
	SOFTLY AS I LEAVE YOU	BALLAD	2'55"	21	DE VITA/ CALABRESE	TRANSL. HARRIS, J	BIG THREE
	MUSIC INTERPOLATED IN STAGE ACTION:						
	JANUARY, FEBRUARY	SONG	3'01"	21	TARNEY, ALAN		ATV MUSIC
	BEER BARREL POLKA, THE	DANCE-SONG	3'00"	21	VEJVODA, J/ ZEMAN, V	TRANSL. BROWN, L/ TIMM, W	KEITH PROWSE
	NEWSTIME	TV JINGLE	10"	21	GOSLING, E/ HOPE, P		INTER-ART CO LTD
	SATIN DOLL	INSTR.	3'00"	21	ELLINGTON/ STRAYHORN/MERCER		CAMPBELL CONNELLY
	IMAGINE	SONG	3'00"	21	LENNON, JOHN		NORTHERN SONGS

SPECIAL NOTE.—It is a condition of the Society's licence that these returns be made, and as the Royalties collected by the Society are distributed in accordance therewith, it is essential that strict accuracy be observed in completing them. Licensees are warned that deliberate falsification of these returns is liable to involve those responsible in serious consequences.

Certified Correct

Signed Walter Plinge

P.T.O.

* Performing Right Society.
* Phonographic Performance.

Returns

All members of the Theatrical Management Association are required to submit monthly returns detailing the number and type of performances given each week. This return is accompanied by a remittance to cover the performance fee which supplements the fixed annual subscription. These performance fees, payable by both producing and theatre operating members, depend on the seating capacity of the auditorium in which the performance is given and are subject to a weekly maximum. Some funding bodies such as the Arts Council require a regular return in a prescribed form. Others merely monitor performance through the papers that they receive as assessors on boards and management committees. All funding bodies, including small district Councils making token contributions, expect a copy of the audited annual accounts.

But possibly the most time-consuming returns are those required by the Performing Right Society detailing every piece of music used: it is upon these figures that they apportion the total sum available for royalty distribution to their members. The PRS does seem to permit some degree of laxity in the making of these returns but they should be undertaken in fairness to the composers . . . and good efficient housekeeping.

Safety

Safety is largely a matter of detailed vigilance with special emphasis on the avoidance of fire risks and the orderly conduct of the theatre, especially when the public are on the premises. A positive approach to safety is a three part process:

(1)   Avoidance of unnecessary risks by organising things in such a way that no foreseeable accident occurs by eliminating all potential sources of danger.

(2)   Being prepared for all contingencies by having available means of restricting the effects of any hazard that suddenly arises without warning.

(3)   Evacuating all persons from the premises in an orderly fashion if circumstances make this necessary.

Particular attention should be given to:

* Allocation of duties for emergency (known as 'Fire Drill', although all emergencies do not necessarily involve fire).
* Advising visiting actors and companies of emergency procedures and any local safety regulations.

* Daily inspection to ensure that there are no obstacles or hazards to the public caused by a lack of building maintenance.
* Regular checks that all fire appliances are serviced and in position and that all members of staff are conversant with their operation.
* Nightly lock up inspection procedures to ensure that overnight fire precautions and security arrangements are operative.
* Ensuring that first aid boxes are replenished and accident record books maintained.
* Stage departmental heads rigidly enforcing backstage fire regulations, particularly in respect of smoking and naked flames.

Maintenance

Every theatre building should have a nominated building surveyor who checks the general structure of the building on a regular basis (wise theatre trusts invite a local property surveyor to become a director!) On a daily basis the housekeeper or head cleaner should report on the following for action to be initiated immediately by the house manager:

* Failed lights.
* Suspicion of gas escape.
* Water system defects.
* Blocked toilets or sink wastes.
* Dripping taps.
* Broken sash cords.
* Broken glass.
* Defective door or window fastenings and hangings.
* Loose or damaged seats and chairs.
* Damaged furniture and upholstery.
* Loose or broken handrails.
* Loose or torn carpet.
* Loose or damaged stair nosings.

When daily cleaning is completed, the following items should be double checked:

* All cleaning materials, vacuum cleaners etc. put away.
* All refuse deposited in dustbins or sacks in such a way that no obstructions are caused.
* All ashtrays emptied and replaced.
* All stair rods and druggets secure.

Communications

It cannot be repeated too frequently that most problems in a theatre arise from lack of communication — up, down and sideways. It is part of general good housekeeping to ensure that everyone knows what is happening: they should not have to resort to speculative gossip or even to the local newspaper. Staff noticeboards, open conversations, involvement, all make a theatre into a happier and safer place to work.

13 Training and recruitment

Formal professional training for theatre workers is relatively new. Musicians, dancers and singers require identifiable skills which a traditional education system is able to devise ways of teaching. To make an objective assessment of an actor's skills is rather more difficult and that is presumably the main reason, apart from the actor's rather late acquisition of respectability, why the drama schools are more recent establishments than the academies of music, ballet, architecture and fine art.

Specialist scene and costume designer training did not really get fully established until the 1950s or even 1960s, and production training has been slowly lumbering into existence over the same period, concentrating at first on stage management, then electrics and only now getting underway to any extent in areas like carpentry, wardrobe and production management.

This is not to say that theatre personnel were previously untrained: merely that until quite recently the training has been practical and informal. The structure has been one of an apprenticeship without formal indentures and with the onus being on the pupil to learn by observation of the master rather than expect to be taught by him.

There were two traditional routes to theatre management. One could start front of house as an office boy and proceed through the box office. Or one could begin backstage and progress through stage management, coming through the pass door in one's forties. Either way one would have acquired a good working knowledge of the required skills. Most theatres were part of a chain which had established management procedures with which one had to conform. The management manual of one leading chain laid down the daily, weekly, monthly and annual procedures for the manager and his assistant. Their life was regulated by printed forms. If anything could be counted, then there was a printed form to be completed with the result of that count. In the unlikely event of a decision being required for which the book made no provision, a telephone call to head office was mandatory.

The rigidity of this system helped to bring about the break up of the circuit controlled theatres. The new locally run theatres required administrators who were equipped to analyse situations and make decisions. If they were to be enablers and motivators, they would require formal apprenticeships in both arts and business procedures. Survival of theatre depends on a shot gun wedding between subjective arts and objective business: no marriage bureau's computer would ever introduce the parties and indeed the divorce rate is rather high!

The emergence of arts administration as a structured career is generally agreed to date from two events: a 1963 initiative by the Council of Repertory Theatres and a 1966 letter to the *Times* by Ian Hunter. Arts Council administration courses started a year later and current policy for selecting and training potential arts administrators stems mainly from a 1971 Arts Council enquiry. The report of that enquiry includes all the basic viewpoints that are still debated, particularly the mix of academic and practical work that is appropriate to both the potential administrator's background and to the training courses. And the degree of specialisation: do we train specialist theatre administrators, gallery administrators, orchestral administrators and so on — or just arts administrators? The debate will continue.

Administration training courses

The principal centre for formal arts administration training in Britain is at the City University in London. The Department of Arts Administration Studies in the City University's Centre for the Arts provides two courses for which the Arts Council is usually able to offer some bursaries for students (overseas students are normally supported by their own government's arts organisation).

Diploma in Arts Administration   This is a one year full-time course for students with some experience in arts administration, normally gained since obtaining a first degree or similar formal qualification. The major areas of study include 'finance, marketing, law and the management of human and physical resources, as well as the ethics of administration of the arts'. The course includes a period of secondment to an arts organisation. The average age of the students is mid to late twenties.

Practical Training Scheme   This course does not have formal education requirements but is intended for those who have had some success in arts administration over two or three years. The scheme is based on a series of secondments, usually to three or four different arts organisations for varying periods over the seven to nine months of the course, plus periods in the university for concentrated study of basic administrative skills and exploration of general arts policy matters.

M.A. in Arts Administration   There is also a two year part-time postgraduate course with students attending for one day per week for four terms then preparing a dissertation during the final two terms.

City University also runs short courses on specialised areas of arts administration including administrative training for production managers. Various universities, polytechnics, and colleges include administrative options in their general arts and theatre courses, and the Association of

British Theatre Technicians is a good source of information on short theatre courses of all kinds.

Anyone contemplating a career in theatre administration should contact the Arts Council's training department for a listing of current courses, suggested reading, and dates of the Arts Council's 'informal open meetings about arts administration courses/schemes' which are held in London from time to time.

Recruitment

As theatre moves increasingly into the area of public accountability, the procedures for recruitment are becoming more formalised. Appointments are increasingly made by selection panels interviewing shortlisted candidates. However, many jobs are still filled by departmental heads informally interviewing a series of applicants until a suitable person is found. *The Stage* is the indispensable place for job adverts and the weekly 'Creative and Media' section of the *Guardian* is a close runner-up. But a lot of vacancies are filled by job hunters who write hopeful letters. Getting a theatre job, particularly a first job, is still very much a matter of being in the right place at the right time. That old cliché 'It's not what you know but who you know' is absolute rubbish. The committed, conscientious and cheerful can always get some kind of theatre work. Add talent and the work offered is proportionately better. Add some charisma and there is no upper limit. Talent is not enough. It is possible, but hard work, to succeed without being cheerful. But without a committed conscientious approach, there is not much point in contemplating a career in theatre admin.

14   Amateur theatre admin

Although this book has concerned itself with the administration of professional theatre, many of the problems discussed will be very familiar to anyone who has been involved in the organisation of an amateur production.

Amateur actors may not be paid but that does not mean that an amateur company is free from financial problems. Survival for an amateur theatre involves organisation, budgets, publicity, and all the rest. Differences from professional theatre are largely a matter of scale. It is convenient to discuss these differences and some other features of amateur theatre under headings used earlier.

Organisation

Very few amateur societies, apart from school and college productions, have their own premises. Most have to rent halls and suffer considerable frustration from lack of time and lack of facilities. Even in the better equipped school halls there can be problems arising from restrictions — either those imposed officially by the authorities as a result of the primary purpose of the building, or those imposed officiously by a guardian caretaker with a special personalised interpretation of the regulations. There is rarely positive obstruction. Passive resistance is more common and the techniques used in overcoming this attitude include cultivating education officers, their drama and music advisers, the headmaster, and that keeper of the technology key, the science master. Some consumption of humble pie, liberal bestowal of thanks and programme credits and a judicious distribution of gratuities are all weapons in the armoury of an amateur theatre administrator seeking to lubricate the path of the society's annual occupation of a rented hall. And all likely to succeed that much more if backed up by an organisation that is not only efficient but gives an impression of efficiency.

Outside the educational system, most amateur societies are constituted in some sort of form that puts decision making in the hands of a committee elected from within the membership. This committee is very similar in structure and function to the boards of directors in a trust controlled professional theatre. And their meeting procedures, agendas, minutes etc. are almost identical.

Staff

Office bearers are appointed and they have a similar function to the professional staff of a theatre. The Hon. Sec. bears the administrative burdens with the support of the Hon. Treasurer, and any Hon. Sec. wishing to survive without tranquillisers should endeavour to recruit a support team to whom some of the areas of work such as house management, box office and publicity can be delegated. The jobs that have to be done in a professional theatre also have to be done in an amateur one — and so the same sort of personnel and skills are required.

Where a company has its own theatre, the organisational responsibility becomes much more detailed and many such societies have found it necessary to have someone giving most of their time (paid or unpaid) to supervising their affairs. For college and university productions included as part of the formal course, there are normally professional facilities available: only the actors are unpaid. But for extra-curricular productions a society structure is required with office bearers to do the production and administrative work.

Funding

The Arts Council and Regional Arts Associations do not normally assist with the funding of amateur productions. However some local authorities give at least token financial assistance while others make premises available at subsidised rentals. Business sponsorship has always been present to some extent in that many firms support drama societies that are formed as part of that firm's recreation and welfare facilities. And a society with a special project, particularly one with local interest, can always approach local industry with some hope. Subsidy can come in ways other than cash: such as a block booking bought for cheap or free distribution to employees.

Then there are annual subscriptions collected from the membership and such supportive events as the bazaars and raffles which form part of the funding activities of all community bodies including the operatic and dramatic ones. Opportunities for auxiliary earned income exist in the programme adverts where local firms, without actually being blackmailed, can be made to feel where their duty lies. And interval coffee becomes profitable if the helpers are unpaid, and more so if they bring along their baking.

But the bulk of funding has to come from seat sales.

Budgeting

A conventional split into production and running costs is probably not necessary and virtually all costs will normally be fixed rather than based on percentages, although the rental terms may include an element of royalty related to box office. The main items of expenditure are likely to be:

*	Physical	Scenery building and painting. Costumes if a period play. Lighting hire if hall not fully equipped. Such props/furniture as cannot be borrowed.
*	Fees	Possibly a professional director for a big musical society. Perhaps also musical director and some orchestra. Author's royalty. Performing Right Society.
*	Advertising	Poster and leaflet printing. Newspaper advertising.
*	Accommodation	Rental of hall. Contra charge for services if renting professional theatre. Rehearsal rooms.
*	Miscellaneous	Ticket printing.

Allow a generous contingency.

Production

Whether a theatre is amateur or professional, the production cannot be directed by a committee. A director has to be appointed and everyone taking part has to agree that this director is right, even when convinced that he is wrong. If disaster is certain, an emergency committee meeting may be held to consider a replacement. But until that point the director must be given dictatorial powers. No decent director, of course, will be seen to use these powers.

The director needs full support and leading that support must be someone who fulfills the function of a production manager. The actual title may be stage manager or it may be one of the hats of the long suffering Hon. Sec. It is the function rather than the title that is important and the function is to ensure that everything required by the staging happens. And happens in time. In an amateur production where time is restricted to evenings and weekends, schedules are even more important (if that is possible) than in professional theatre.

Publicity

Publicity is vital and needs a good share of the budget to pay for decent posters and an advertising campaign in the local papers. It is much easier for an amateur company to get its posters displayed. Not only does the society have its contacts with the local businesses but shops are happy to support community efforts, not without half an eye on the commercial advantage to be gained from obliging customers. The local council is often much happier about sanctioning banners across the street to advertise an amateur production than a professional one.

The local paper will allocate more editorial space, but this valuable perk must not be abused. Give them decently typed information and insist that the cast stop rehearsing to pose when the press photographer comes at the appointed time. There should be no difficulties in getting windows for a display of photographs of the well known local personalities taking part. The local paper will be happy to send a critic since quite a lot of its readers are either in the show, connected with it, or related to it. It is news. The critic may well be an apprentice reporter: handle carefully, they often have an ambitious pen. And ambitious cub reporters can be lethal if they want to make their mark.

Selling seats

An amateur society playing in a hired hall rarely has the facilities of a permanent box office. Advance tickets may be sold through a local shop such as a travel agent who handles concert bookings. However society members may have to do some face-to-face selling among their friends. Probably not a lot of scope for reductions, special offers and all these kinds of marketing ploys. But there is a lot to be said for two-for-one on the opening night.

Playing in professional theatres

Many societies, particularly the bigger operatic societies, perform in their local theatres or arts centres. Indeed in many community theatres, amateurs have a very positive role to play in making possible performances that would otherwise be impossible because of the large numbers of people involved. When playing in such theatres, societies have all the backstage and front of house facilities available to them. Backstage there will be the benefits of technical staff and equipment, while in front the administrative machine will be available in the way that it is to any other touring company. This includes box office facilities and promotion as part of the season through participation in seasonal posters and diary brochures.

There are a number of points that a society should watch in its dealings with a host professional theatre:

*   Appoint one person as liaison with the theatre's administration, and one person as liaison with the theatre's technical management.
*   Ensure that the theatre's technical staff have adequate advance infor-

mation on stage requirements and the proposed schedule. In particular, safety and fire precautions should be discussed and appropriate steps taken in designing the scenery and props.

* Actors and stage staff should use the stage door and must never appear in the public areas in costume or make-up; and they should conform to any other backstage regulations which will be displayed on noticeboards and in the dressing rooms.

* Read the contract carefully: this will prevent any unpleasant surprises when the time comes to settle up financially.

* Submit programme copy and advertising details well before the deadline, preferably typed with double spacing on one side of the paper only.

* Discuss advertising and publicity arrangements with the theatre's promotional staff. Supply photographs and information as early as possible for foyer displays.

* If there are to be special ticket arrangements such as priority booking for members, concessions etc., seek an early meeting with the box office manager to discuss details. Keep the arrangements simple and don't change the rules half way through the booking period.

* A responsible identifiable member of the society should be on duty in the foyer 45 minutes prior to curtain time and should be available in the front of house area throughout the performance.

Audience care

If playing in a professional theatre, do not leave all the audience care to the resident house manager and staff. Behave as you would if you were in a hall without these resident extra people. Have officers of the society in the foyer to smile upon the audience, welcoming them and saying good night. Remember to entertain the mayor and his entourage and make an occasion of Civic Night: it is the chairman's duty to escort His Worship to his seat, unless of course the chairman is the leading actor. Try to arrange for a good photographic display, including past productions.

Training

Consider the possibility of the summer week and all the year round weekend courses that are run at national and local level. If they are in short supply, or do not include the required subjects, have a word with the local education authority's drama adviser. Make your members more aware of the need for administration and its problems by including occasional talks on the subject in your annual programme of 'club nights'. The manager and perhaps the box office manager of your local theatre might welcome an invitation to explain how they work.

. . . . and finally . . .

Whether amateur or professional, it's all about smiling, budgeting, smiling; scheduling, smiling, assuming that if something can happen it will, smiling, trying to stop that awful something actually happening, smiling, but being ready for disaster, smiling, attention to detail, smiling, but being ready for disaster, smiling, attention to detail, smiling. And if once a week you have a day when none of the cast look daggers at you, there is a chance that you are probably winning.

Glossary

In addition to standard administration words and phrases, some of the more frequently used backstage terms and job titles have been included in this glossary.

Advance   (1) Tickets sold to members of the audience who book their seats 'in advance' rather than wait to buy them at the 'doors' (q.v.) on arrival for the performance.
(2) The money held for performances yet to take place.

Alternative theatre   Originally known as 'fringe theatre'. Sets out to offer an experimental alternative to the more formal mainstream theatre and create a new audience in the process. The best of these alternative ideas and ideals are continuously being absorbed by mainstream theatres, allowing fresh alternatives to develop.

Angel   An individual who backs a commercial production by investing money in it.

Apron   A part of the stage projecting towards or into the auditorium. In proscenium stages, the part of the stage in front of the main house curtain.

Artistic director   The person responsible for programme structure and performance standards.

A.S.M.   Assistant stage manager.

Backer's audition   A gathering for prospective investors to hear the details of the plot of a projected production. Mostly held for musicals so that some of the numbers can be performed to encourage investment.

Backing   (1) The money invested in a commercial production.
(2) Piece of scenery behind a door, window, fireplace or similar opening.

Band call   Any orchestral rehearsal but particularly a musical (i.e. non-acting) rehearsal of performers with orchestra.

Billing   The order of prominence on posters and other advertising material given to the names of the various people associated with a production. Size and position is included in individual contracts and determined by negotiation.

Board   (1) Contraction of switchboard or dimmerboard: the central control point for stage lighting.
(2) The directors who constitute the management committee of a company.

Book   The storyline and the words other than lyrics in a musical show.

Boom   Vertical scaffolding pole for mounting lighting instruments.

Borders   Neutral or designed strips of material hung horizontally above the stage to form a limit to the scene and mask the technical regions above the performance area.

Box office   (1) The point of sale of theatre tickets.
(2) Income from the sale of tickets.

Box office card   A poster of size approx 10 × 15 inches, printed on stiff card and provided with a cord for hanging.

Box set   Naturalistic setting of complete room with only the side nearest the audience (the 'fourth wall') missing. Often complete with ceiling.

Bridge   An access catwalk passing across the stage or the auditorium ceiling — usually for lighting. Also used to describe stage floor sections which can be raised or lowered.

Bump out   Australasian term for get-out(q.v.).

Bus and truck   N. American term for a tour specially designed for short stops (often one, two or three nights).

Business   (1) The theatre as a whole i.e. 'The Business', presumably shortened from 'showbusiness'.
(2) The degree of success at the box office i.e. 'How is the business'.
(3) Moves and actions which are added to the script in rehearsal, particularly 'comedy business'.

Call   (1) A notification of a working session (e.g. rehearsal call).
(2) A request for an actor to come to the stage as his entrance is imminent (formerly by call boy, now by dressing room loudspeakers).
(3) An acknowledgment of applause (i.e. curtain call).

Call board   A notice board near the stage door upon which all notices for the production are posted, including 'calls' for rehearsals and performances.

Cans   Headset of earphones, usually with boom microphone, used for communications between stage management and technicians.

Capitalisation   The total sum of invested money required to produce a commercial production.

Casting director   The person who suggests possible suitable actors for the director and producer to audition for the various parts.

Casuals   Temporary staff, usually part-time.

CCTC   Closed circuit television used to transmit picture of stage to audience latecomers waiting in foyer. Also used to transmit picture of conductor in orchestra pit to off-stage singers.

Censorship   A process by which only officially sanctioned scripts may be performed. Abandoned in Britain in 1968.

Classified   Regular newspaper advertising appearing in a fixed format in a fixed position familiar to readers in search of information about current and forthcoming entertainments.

Close   The end of a run ('We close on Saturday').

Cloth   A large area of scenic canvas hanging vertically. A 'backcloth' completes the rear of a scene. A 'frontcloth' hangs well downstage usually to hide a scene change taking place behind.

Cobos   Tickets awaiting collection at the box office (i.e. 'care of box office').

Commercial   Productions where the funding is supplied by investors who hope that the production will be sufficiently successful not only to repay their capital but to distribute profits large enough to compensate for the high risk involved.

Comps   Tickets issued free with the 'compliments' of the theatre.

Contra   An account for services and materials incurred by a theatre on behalf of a producing management. Normally settled by witholding from the producing manager's share of the box office receipts.

Copy   Text supplied to the printer for inclusion in programmes, leaflets, etc.

Cover   A term used, particularly in opera, for a standby or understudy actor.

Cue   The signal that initiates a change of any kind during a performance.

Dark   A theatre which is temporarily or permanently closed to the public.

Dayman   Permanent full time 'rank and file' member of the technical staff, e.g. stage dayman, electrics dayman.

Day seats   Seats not available in advance but retained for sale on the day of performance only.

Designer   Responsible for conception, and supervision of the execution of the visual aspects of the production. Separate designers may be employed for scenery, costumes, and lighting.

Director   Has the ultimate responsibility for the interpretation of the script through his control of the actors and supporting production team.

Displays   (1) Large newspaper adverts giving a more detailed selling message to back up the summary information in the classified adverts.

(2) Photographs, posters, etc. displayed on the front of the theatre and in the foyer to encourage ticket sales for current and forthcoming productions.

Doors   (1) Seats sold immediately prior to the performance rather than in advance.

(2) The total money received for such sales at each performance.

Double crown   A poster of size 20 × 30 inches.

Downstage   The part of the stage nearest to the audience.

Dramatists' Guild   The professional society in America that negotiates the minimum contractual terms between producers and playwrights, librettists, lyricists and composers.

Dresser   Helps actors with costume care and costume changing during the performance.

Dressing (the set)   Decorative (i.e. non-functional) items added to a stage setting.

Dressing the house   Selling seats in such a way that the auditorium looks fuller than it actually is.

Dress parade   Prior to the first stage dress rehearsal, the actors put on each of their costumes in sequence so that the director and designer can check the state of preparedness of the wardrobe department.

Dry   An actor forgetting the words of the script.

False proscenium   A portal (q.v.), particularly one in the downstage area.

False stage   A special temporary stage floor laid for a production to allow scenery trucks, guided by tracks cut into the floor, to be moved by steel wires running in the shallow (two or three inches) void between the false and original stage floors.

Final return   Summary of the total seat sales for a performance.

First call   A variation of the percentage system in touring contracts when the visiting company does not receive a guaranteed minimum share but is entitled to (i.e. has first call on) a stipulated amount providing that the box office receipts actually reach that figure — or to whatever lesser sum is reached.

Fit up   (1) The initial assembly on the stage of a production's hardware including the hanging of scenery, building of trucks etc., and the installation of production lighting (the electrics fit up).

(2) An older name for a barnstorming company who could adapt to playing in halls and improvised theatres of all types.

Flats Lightweight timber frames covered with scenic canvas. Now often covered with plywood and consequently no longer light. When dropped into position from the flys, known as 'french flats'.

Float (1) A sum of money in small denomination notes and coins which enables change to be available from the daily commencement of business in a selling operation.

(2) Jargon for footlights.

Flys The area above the stage into which scenery can be hoisted out of sight of the audience.

Fly floor High working platforms at the sides of the stage from which the flying lines are handled.

Flyman Technician who operates the scenery suspension system above the stage.

Fly tower High structure above the stage which contains the flys(q.v.)

Focus The process of adjusting the beams of spotlights and the directions in which they point.

Fold The end of a run ('The show folded last Saturday').

Foldback Sound reinforcement from loudspeakers facing the actors to enable them to hear their musical accompaniments clearly, and to hear their own and each other's voices when the sound is heavily reinforced for the audience.

Follow spots Spotlights used with an operator to follow actors around the stage.

Forestage The area in front of the house curtain on a proscenium stage.

Free sheet A newspaper with a high advertising content distributed without charge to every address in a specified area.

Fringe see alternative theatre.

Front of house (1) Everything on the audience side of the proscenium.

(2) The spotlights situated on the audience side of the proscenium.

Front cloth (1) A cloth (q.v) hanging at the front of the stage.

(2) A variety act which can perform in the shallow depth of stage in front of a frontcloth.

Get out (1) The dismantling and removal of the physical production from the stage at the end of the run.

(2) The minimum weekly box office receipts that will cover the production expenses to the point of breaking even.

Ghost walks Treasury call — the paying out of weekly salaries.

Grants Subsidy or sponsorship contributions of a predetermined amount which is not dependent on the financial outcome of the performances which they are intended to assist. (see also guarantee)

Green The part of the stage visible to the audience.

Green room Room adjacent to the stage (i.e. the 'green') for the actors to meet and relax.

Gross The total amount of money taken at the theatre box office — normally for one week.

Guarantee   Subsidy or sponsorship contributions to cover the actual extent of any loss incurred up to a nominated amount (see also grants).

Half   A call given to the actors half an hour before they will be called to the stage for the beginning of the performance. Given 35 minutes before the advertised time of commencement. (Subsequent calls are 'the quarter', 'five minutes' and 'beginners').

Hallkeeper   Stage door keeper.

H.O.D.   Head of Department, particularly a theatre's resident stage manager, master carpenter and chief electrician.

Hot ticket   A very successful show for which seats are in heavy demand.

Housekeeper   Supervisor of a theatre's cleaning staff.

Houselights   The decorative lighting in the auditorium.

House seats   Seats held back by the box office for possible use by important or influential visitors. They are released for sale shortly before the performance if it becomes apparent that they will not be required for this purpose.

Intendant   A German title for the person responsible for all artistic and business aspects of a theatre's operation.

Impresario   A producer. Usually reserved for one who operates with a considerable degree of individuality and flamboyance.

Industrial show   A staged production to promote a manufactured product: particularly the launching of a new product to the salesmen and agents of the manufacturing company.

Ladder   Framework in the shape of a ladder for hanging spotlights.

Legs   Vertical strips of fabric used mainly for masking — either decorative or neutral.

Libraries   Ticket agencies, especially in London, who have an allocation of seats for which they charge a booking fee to the customer in addition to obtaining a commission from the theatre.

Licensee   The individual nominated to hold the theatre's licences (Theatres Act, Magistrates, etc).

Limes   Jargon for follow spots (qv) and their operators.

Line printer   The part of a computerised box office installation which produces printed returns plus accounting and statistical reports on request.

Linkman   An old term falling out of use for attendants, particularly those who tore tickets.

Load out   American term for get out (q.v.).

Logo   A graphic symbol used as a design feature in publicity to give continuity and improve identification.

Master carpenter   Senior member of the scenery staff in a theatre. Also senior carpenter in the workshops.

Matter   The written information to be printed on a poster or programme.

Matured   The advance sales for today's performance.

Mechanist   Alternative term (particularly Australasia) for stage carpenter and stage hand — i.e. the technicians responsible for scenery handling.

Middle range salary levels   A formula agreed between TMA and Equity whereby experienced non-star actors receive salaries above the contractual minimum.

Mixed programme theatre   A theatre without its own producing company which presents touring musical and dramatic entertainment of all kinds.

Mixer   Desk for controlling the quality, quantity, and balance of electronically processed sound.

Moving the line   Altering the row at which seat prices change in order to take account of fluctuations in the demand for tickets.

Moving the rope   see Moving the line

MRSL   See Middle range salary levels.

M.D.   Musical Director or Conductor.

Notice   (1) A press review of a production.
(2) The announcement posted on the call board (q.v.) giving the date of the end of a production's run and formally terminating all 'run-of-the-show' contracts from the date.

Off   An actor who misses his entrance.

O.P.   Opposite Prompt side of the stage — i.e. stage right (actor's right when facing the audience).

Open   Seats which are unsold.

Option   An agreement with a playwright giving the holder the exclusive right to produce the play within a stipulated period of time.

Overheads   Costs other than those arising from the presentation of specific productions.

Paper   Complimentary tickets.

Pass door   The door from the auditorium to the stage (usually small because it is in the all-important 'fire wall'). Passage, particularly during performances, is restricted by rules and customs to a small number of essential users.

Pencil   Dates held available for a production to play in a theatre subject to further negotiation and contract.

Photo call   A session for the purpose of taking production and/or press photographs.

Physical production   The costs involved in providing all the material for the stage environment i.e. the scenery building and painting, furniture and set dressing, properties, costume.

Piano dress   Rehearsal in costume and with all technical facilities but using piano as a substitute for orchestra so that the director can concentrate on movement and technical problems rather than musical ones.

Playbill   Free Broadway theatre programmes funded solely by advertising.

Plot   A listing of preparations and actions required during a performance. Each staging department prepares such plots as are required by the individual department's members.

Preset   Anything which is positioned in advance of its being required — such as props placed on the set before the performance, or a scene set behind a backcloth, or a lighting or sound control desk with facilities to set balances in advance of a cue.

Press release   A written information announcement circulated to the media.

Preview   A performance, usually at reduced prices, given prior to the formal opening night attended by the press.

Producer   Formerly the person who directed the actors. Now the packager who brings together script, theatre, production team, possibly the star(s) and certainly the money.

Product   A general term covering performances of all possible types.

Production desk   Portable table with lights and communication systems used by the production team in the auditorium during rehearsals.

Production manager   Responsible for the technical preparation, including budgeting of new productions.

Project funding   Subsidy earmarked for a specific production or a definite activity such as a marketing campaign (see also Revenue).

PS   Prompt side of the stage — stage left (actor's left when facing the audience).

Prompt book   Master copy of the script containing all actor moves and technical cues, used by the stage management to control the performance.

Property   A script, score or perhaps just even an idea or title from which it is hoped that a production will develop. Someone usually holds an option (q.v.) on it.

Properties   Furnishings, set-dressings, and all items large and small which cannot be classified as scenery, electrics or wardrobe.

Proscenium theatre   The traditional form of theatre where the audience sit in a single block facing the stage with a fairly definite division between audience and stage. The position of this division is known as the proscenium and takes many forms from a definite arch, not unlike a picture frame, to an unstressed termination of the auditorium walls and ceiling.

Pull   To remove a ticket from the ticket book. Normally only done when the sale is confirmed and payment received.

Pyrotechnics   Bombs, bangs, flashes etc., usually fired electrically. Strict safety precautions required, some of which are mandatory. Consult ABTT Code of Practice (see booklist).

Recoupment   The point when a production has recovered its total investment capital.

Reinforcement   Increasing the level of sound by electronic amplification.

Repertoire   A form of organisation where two or more productions alternate in the course of a week's performances.

Repertory   A form of organisation, usually with a permanent company of actors, where each production has a run of limited length. At any time there is normally one production in performance, another in rehearsal and several in varying degrees of planning.

Repetiteur   Pianist and vocal coach in an opera house.

Residency   A touring company operating from a temporary regional base over a short concentrated period to give performances and associated workshops in the surrounding area.

Resident stage manager   Title given, mainly in touring theatres, to the master carpenter. Responsible to the theatre manager for the staff and the building, and to the touring manager for provision of performance facilities.

Return   (1) A statistical statement, particularly a statement of tickets sold and money taken, by the box office.
(2) Tickets returned to the box office for resale.
Revenue funding   Subsidy contributions towards general operating expenses. (see also project funding).
Review   A newspaper or magazine's critical assessment of a production.
Revue   A production compiled from a series of musical and comedy items.
Road   Going on tour. In America, the entire nation outside New York City.
Road manager (roadie)   A touring technician with one-night-stands, particularly music groups.
Run   A sequence of performances of the same production.
Runners   A pair of curtains parting at the centre and running horizontally, particularly those used in the downstage position in variety and revue productions.
Scene dock   High ceilinged storage area adjacent to the stage.
Scenographer   The accepted international term for the designer(s) who provide the visual environment for the actor. Implies a theatre where the environment is an integral constituent of the production rather than a decorative addition.
Seatway   The measurement (for licensing and safety purposes) between the back of one seat and the foremost portion of the one behind.
Secondary lighting   Lighting maintained by batteries which provides sufficient illumination to evacuate the theatre in safety if the main electricity supply fails.
Segue   Musical term for an immediate follow on. Often used as jargon for any kind of immediate follow on.
Showman   Part time member of technical staff engaged for performances only.
Sightlines   Lines drawn on plan and section to indicate limits of audience vision from extreme seats, including side seats and front and back rows.
Sitzprobe   Opera house term for a rehearsal with orchestra where the cast sing but do not act.
Sponsorship   Income awarded from private or industrial funds to cover the deficit between costs and earned income (see also subsidy).
Sprinklers   Devices which release water automatically in the event of fire.
Staff director   Member of the production staff in a repertoire theatre responsible for maintaining the standard of a production in the repertoire, including revivals and cast changes. Usually was the assistant director on the original rehearsals of the production.
Stage director   Formerly the senior member of the stage mangement team but title now rarely used in order to avoid confusion with the director.
Stage manager   In overall control of the performance with responsibility for signalling the cues that coordinate the work of the actors and technicians. Some of this responsibility is delegated to the deputy stage manager (DSM) and the assistant stage manager(s) (ASM).
Stage wait   A delay in the rise of the curtain or an interruption to the flow of the performance caused by an actor drying(q.v), being off(q.v.) or a problem with a scene change.
Stagione   A form of repertoire with a very small range of productions in performance at any given time. Each production is given intense rehearsal followed by a

burst of performances close together, then placed in store. Revivals are rehearsed almost as if they were new productions.

Standing   (1)Scenery ('standing set') or lights ('standing light') which does not change during the performance.

(2) Spaces sold for audience to stand when all seats are sold. Numbers and positions are strictly determined by licensing authorities.

Standby   (1) A principal understudy who may play some matinees in a tiring show.

(2) Tickets sold at a reduced price immediately before the performance starts. May be general standby or, more commonly restricted to a category, especially students.

Straight   Non-musical — i.e. 'straight play', 'straight actor'.

Stub   The portion of a ticket retained by the box office for accounting purposes.

Subscription   Booking a series of performances to obtain an assured seat and a discount.

Subsidiary rights   Royalties arising from a production other than from performances in major theatres, i.e. amateur, film, TV, merchandising etc.

Subsidy   Income awarded from public funds to cover the deficit between costs and earned income (see also sponsorship).

Tabs   Originally 'tableaux curtains' which drew outwards and upwards, but now generally applied to any curtain including a vertically flying front curtain (house tabs) and especially a pair of horizontally moving curtains which overlap at centre and move outwards from that centre.

Technical director (administrator/manager)   Coordinates and budgets the work of all technical departments.

Terminal   The unit which gives access to the memorised seating plans of a computerised box office. By means of a keyboard any plan may be selected and seats allocated. There is normally also a ticket printer to produce the ticket at the moment of sale.

Theatres Act   A 1968 act controlling a theatre's operation, mainly in respect of public safety standards, by making performances subject to the issue of a licence by the local authority.

Theatre in Education (TIE)   A touring company, often attached to a regional theatre, who perform in schools.

Theatre-in-the-round   A form of staging where the audience totally encircle the acting area.

Throw   The distance between a light and the actor or object being lit.

Throwaway   (1) A small advertising leaflet.

(2) A line in the script which the actors deliver without emphasis or meaning.

Thrust   Form of stage which projects into the auditorium so that the audience are seated on at least two sides.

Ticket printer   The unit in a computerised box office which prints the ticket at the moment of sale.

Tony Award   The Broadway theatre's most prestigious awards.

Topping & tailing   Cutting out the dialogue and action between cues in a technical rehearsal.

Tormentors   Narrow masking flats at right angles to the proscenium.

Tumbling Flying a cloth from the bottom as well as the top when there is insufficient height to fly in the normal way.

Twofer Two seats for the price of one.

Upstage (1) The part of the stage furthest from the audience.
(2) An old technique, but not entirely unknown today, whereby one actor out maneouvres another in securing a commanding position on the stage.

Venue A place where a performance takes place.

Wardrobe General name for the costume department, its staff, and the accommodation that they occupy.

Wardrobe maintenance The division of the wardrobe department responsible for the day-to-day cleaning, pressing and running repairs.

Wardrobe plot Actor-by-actor, scene-by-scene, inventory of all the costumes in a production giving a detailed breakdown into every separate item in each costume.

Week out A week in the middle of a tour when performances are suspended because no suitable theatre is available.

Theatre organisations

Organisations referred to in text

Arts Administration Studies Centre for the Arts, The City University, Northampton Square, London EC1V 0HB   01-253-4399.
The Arts Council of Great Britain 105 Piccadilly, London W1V 0AU   01-629-9495.
Association for Business Sponsorship of the Arts (ABSA) 12 Abbey Churchyard, Bath BA1 1LY   0225-63762.
British Actors Equity Association 8 Harley Street, London W1N 2AB   01-636-6367.
Federation of Playgoers Societies Hon. Sec: c/o 27 The Common, Colchester, Essex.
Independent Theatre Council (ITC) Top Floor, McArthur Warehouse, Gas Ferry Road, Bristol BS1 6UN   0272-685047.
London Theatre Council Communications re Managers: The Joint Secretary, Bedford Chambers, Covent Garden, London WC2   (01-836-0971). Communications re artists: The Joint Secretary, 8 Harley Street, London W1   01-636 6737.
Mechanical Copyright Protection Society Elgar House, 41 Streatham High Road, London SW16 1ER
Musician's Union 60/62 Clapham Road, London SW9 0JJ
National Association of Theatrical, Television and Kine Employees (NATTKE) 155 Kennington Park Road, London SE11 4JU   01-735-9068.
Office of Arts and Libraries Department of Education and Science, Elizabeth House, York Road, London SE1 7PH   01-928-9222.
Performing Right Society Ltd 29/33 Berners Street, London W1P 4AA 01-580-5544.
Phonographic Performance Ltd 14 Ganton Street, London W1V 1LB   01-437-0311.
Provincial Theatre Council Communications re managers and artists should be made to the same addresses as for the London Theatre Council.
Society of West End Theatre (SWET) Bedford Chambers, Covent Garden, London WC2   01-836-0971.
Theatre Investment Fund 18/20 Maiden Lane, Strand, London WC2   01-836-9245.

Theatrical Management Association (TMA) (incorporating the Council of Regional Theatre and the Association of Touring and Producing Managers) Bedford Chambers, Covent Garden, London WC2   01-836-0971.
Theatres National Committee Bedford Chambers, Covent Garden, London WC2   01-836-0971.
The Theatres Trust 10 St Martin's Court, St Martin's Lane, London WC2N 4AJ.
Theatre Writers' Union (TWU) 9 Fitzroy Square, London W1   01-387-2666
Writers' Guild of Great Britain 430 Edgware Road, London W2 1EH   01-723-8074.

Some other organisations

Association of British Theatre Technicians 4 Great Pulteney Street, London W1R 3DF Tel. 01-434-3901. An association of all those who assist the actor in his performance. Membership includes architects, administrators, directors, designers, technicians and equipment manufacturers. Organises training courses and through a system of specialist committees publishes advisory documents including suggested codes of practice for the technical aspects of theatre operation.
British Council 10 Spring Gardens, London SW1A 2BN Tel. 01-930-8466. As part of its mandate to develop cultural relations between Britain and other countries, the British Council organises overseas tours by British theatre companies. It also organises some overseas lecturing and assists with travel funding for individuals visiting countries with whom cultural exchanges might otherwise be limited.
Council of Regional Arts Associations (CORAA) 59 St James's Street, London SW1A 1LL Tel. 01-629-9586. An association of the officers of the Regional Arts Associations.
Institute of Leisure and Amenity Management (ILAM) Lower Basildon, Reading, Berks. Incorporating the Institute of Municipal Entertainment, ILAM is the professional body for theatre administrative staff in the leisure services and entertainments departments of local authorities.
Society of Theatre Consultants 4 Great Pulteney Street, London W1R 3DF Tel. 01-434-3904. The professional association of advisers on the specialist nature of theatre architecture, whether new building or refurbishment.
Stage Management Association 81 St Mary's Grove, London W4 3LW Tel. 01-994-5261. Circulates to managers, on request, a monthly list of members available for engagements.
Standing Advisory Committee on Local Authorities and the Arts (SACLAT) 25 Buckingham Gate, London SW1E 6LE. Provides a link

between the local authorities and the theatre industry, particularly through a series of seminars dealing with various aspects of theatre development and administration.

Theatres Advisory Council 4 Great Pulteney Street, London W1R 3DF Tel. 01-434-3901. With a membership comprising most of the theatre organisations the TAC is particularly concerned with maintaining the provision of theatre buildings throughout the United Kingdom.

The Theatre Museum Room 132, The Victoria and Albert Museum, South Kensington, London SW7 2RL Tel. 01-589-6371. The collections are currently available only on a restricted basis to specialist researchers, but there are plans for an accessible Theatre Museum to open eventually in the Flower Market, Covent Garden.

The Theatrical Traders Association Ltd 21/2 York Street, Twickenham, Middlesex TW1 3LA Tel. 01-892-6245. A trade association to assist, protect and promote suppliers of goods and services to theatres and theatrical producers.

Variety and Allied Entertainments Council of Great Britain 403 Collingwood House, Dolphin Square, London SW1V 3NE Tel. 01-834-0515 and 8 Harley Street London W1N 2AB Tel. 01-636-6367. Regulates the relations between managers, agents, and artists engaged in variety and allied fields.

Some suggestions for further reading

ABTT Codes of Practice for the Theatre Industry The Association of British Theatre Technicians is engaged on the preparation of a series of suggested codes of practice for both backstage and front of house management. Of those already published, *Advice on Standards for Occasional Licences* (1981) is particularly valuable.

Annual Reports of the Arts Council of Great Britain All you want to know about who gets how much.

Amateur Stage (Stacey Publications) Monthly. News, features and reviews.

Arts Administration John Pick (E & F.N. Spon 1980) An overview of the general principles involved in the administration of all the visual and performing arts. Much of the book is about funding: particularly the role of the state.

British Alternative Theatre Directory (John Offord Publications) Annual listings of alternative theatre companies, venues, playwrights, directors, designers, organisations, etc. Indispensable.

British Theatre Directory (John Offord Publications) Another indispensable annual reference.

The Case for Arts Centres (John Offord Publications 1981) Entertaining explanation of the nature and purpose of arts centres in all their forms.

Contacts (Published annually by the Spotlight Ltd) Concise listings of the names, addresses and telephone numbers of theatres, managements, agents, etc.

The TMA Marketing Manual Four volumes edited by Glyn V. Robbins and Peter Verwey. (John Offord Publications). Specialist essays on such subjects as marketing, print, press relations, mailing lists, concessions, audience research, advertising, display, etc.

Entertainment and Arts Management (John Offord Publications) Monthly. Illustrated round up of news on management topics, particularly strong on municipally operated venues and the companies who specialise in supplying them with products.

From Option to Opening Donald C. Farber (Drama Book Specialists, New York 1977) The nuts and bolts of producing Off-Broadway.

Performance Leslie E. Cotterell (John Offord Publications 1977) Discusses the legal implications of agreements, contracts, copyright, licensing and Acts of Parliament upon the theatre and all performance situations.

Producing on Broadway: A comprehensive guide Donald C. Farber (Drama Book Specialists, New York 1969). It's exactly what the title says.

The Stage (Carson & Comerford Ltd) Every Thursday. The indispensable newspaper. Absolutely indispensable.

The Staging Handbook Francis Reid (A & C Black, London and Theatre Arts Books, New York 1978). An introduction to the work of the backstage departments and the procedures involved in staging plays, musicals, opera, dance, tours, etc.

Theatre Business: From auditions through opening night Jan Weingarten Greenberg (Holt, Rinehart and Winston, New York 1981). The author, a New York theatrical press agent describes Broadway as if it were a sane, relaxed smoothly run business. Some interesting budget figures, but mainly an entertaining introduction to Donald C. Farber's more detailed treatments.

Theatre at Work. The story of the National Theatre's production of Brecht's Galileo Jim Hiley (Routledge & Kegan Paul 1981). Follows the 22 weeks of preparation of a no-expense-spared production in a major theatre.

Theatre in Europe John Allen (John Offord Publications 1981) Interesting information on the financing of drama theatres in Western Europe.

Theatre Inside Out Kenneth Hurren (W.H. Allen, 1977). An entertaining gossipy look at aspects of the London theatre scene, including some useful financial facts which are still useful if inflation adjusted.

Training Arts Administrators. Report of the Committee of Enquiry into Arts Administrator Training (Arts Council of Great Britain 1971) The document which formalised the concept of Arts Administration as a profession and established the educational programmes which form the basis of current training and recruitment policy.

Variety The American showbiz weekly. The motion picture, music and video sections tend to overshadow the 'legitimate' theatre section, but this however is full of the facts that anyone interested in theatre admin just loves to read: the box office results for all current New York shows and major tours. Oh, that Britain's theatre world would have the courage to release their weekly figures for publication in *Stage!*

Index

Page numbers in **BOLD** refer to glossary